What You Can Do About . . .

Inflation
Unemployment
Productivity
Profit
and
Collective Bargaining

By
Lemuel R. Boulware

LOEFFLER & CO., INC.
Box 9622
San Diego, California 92109

What You Can Do About
Inflation
Unemployment
Productivity
Profit (and)
Collective Bargaining

Printed in the United States of America

CONTENTS

PREFACE

In my twelfth year of retirement, I was as pleased as surprised to receive out of the blue an invitation to conduct a series of lectures and discussions at Florida Atlantic University's School of Business and Public Administration in association with the American Society for Personnel Administration.

With the wage-price spiral and the inroads of foreign competition bringing collective bargaining into fresh focus, the subject initially suggested was what may be ailing the negotiating process, what contribution this may be making to the current inflation, unemployment, productivity and profit problems, and who should be doing what in the circumstances.

But in trying to prepare for the lectures, and then in the class room discussions, it became very evident that the real question was what should *everybody* be learning and doing toward resolving the *overall* inflation, unemployment, productivity and profit crisis and how, as one characteristic step toward that end, should everybody be trying to help collective bargaining contribute to that resolution and be otherwise as good in practice as it is good in concept.

Accordingly, this inquiry extends to what the public majority, at all levels, may need to do not only as to its own ideas and acts but also as to the instructions or permissions that majority gives its formally or informally appointed agents in unions, business and government.

The class consisted entirely of Master of Business Administration candidates who were on campus for one of their periodic stays. Most of the class were neither in union relations work nor engaged elsewhere in the personnel area.

What seemed their biggest surprise was my emphasis on the job-connected and citizenship-connected responsibility of each of them, on and off the job, for corrective thought-leadership in the presently so neglected subjects which bear on the individual's interest in what happens not just at the bargaining table but elsewhere.

Especially hard to accept in the beginning was my insistence that the farther away from the actual bargaining they individually were—in or out of the personnel area—the greater was their obligation to themselves and others to exercise such leadership.

Approximately an hour's scrutiny and challenge by the class followed each initial presentation. This book attempts to summarize the lectures as since edited in the light of those discussions.

As only to be expected, the views expressed are often different from those usually encountered, for otherwise there would have been no occasion for the lectures. These views are reported here not as anything authorative or final but in the hope they may serve as a somewhat useful stimulant to abler individuals than I among that wider audience of the presently and potentially available thought leaders now so desperately needed not only in how to surmount our current crisis but also in how to maximize free choice, private property and limited government in the process.

8

Incidentally, I take no compensation from the book but offer my part in it as a public service in making possible the lower price and wider readership. This is in recognition—even at age 77—of a still unmet obligation imposed by the opportunities and rewards that have come my way.

And in case any such claimed unselfishness should sound a little too noble, I confess in addition the very selfish urge arising from the fact that my mother lived to 103 and that I am sure, unless there is a big change in direction, both the reader and I are not going to like what we find down my remaining 26 years.

Lemuel R. Boulware

New York
June, 1972

Chapter I

MY THESIS

Every thoughtful student of our economic scene must be concerned that so much seems to have suddenly gone so wrong with the system which has given man his best 200 years.

Obviously a considerable part of that concern now extends not only to why the collective bargaining process, which is so perfectly good in theory, seems to have gone so far astray not only in practice but also to who is and is not doing what needs to be done about it.

I believe whatever may ail collective bargaining is not inherent in the process itself but is due to the negligence of citizens on whose authority it proceeds and whose interests are at stake as concurrent workers, consumers and savers—in short, just about everybody several times over.

More importantly, I believe that any bargaining problems arc just some of the outcroppings of a much deeper problem to which the public majority needs to address itself for many more urgent reasons than just those connected with negotiations. To illustrate, I believe:

1. What is *outwardly* the matter with bargaining is that there is actually so little of it in the

sense of the negotiation between equals which most voters originally intended and which most citizens still wrongly assume is what goes on.

2. This miscarriage is due to the customary but seldom admitted weakness of management representatives in contrast to the overwhelming but not publicly sensed strength of the union representatives involved.

3. This imbalance of power is, in turn, due in large measure to the way bargaining has been permitted to depart from its purely economic and working-condition goals and to become almost solely a *political* process. As a consequence, and as is usual in politics elsewhere, the representatives so often must or can do what is bad for, but will look good to, their inadequately informed and alerted constituents.

4. The resulting damage to worker, consumer and saver interests alike is not *primarily* the fault of union, business or government *representatives,* but is *basically* the fault of *what the public majority is doing to itself* both through its own direct acts as individuals and through what it instructs or permits its various agents to do.

5. The very same mistaken ideas and actions, which are troubling collective bargaining, are having even more serious consequences over a much wider field. Thus our current crisis has put us in a desperate race between re-education and disaster. It therefore behooves every citizen to do his individual best to re-examine at once his *ideas* for any futile wishful thinking, his *emotions* for any ill-advised and selfdamaging prejudices, his *actions* for any impractical and immoral guests, and his *agents* in unions, business

and government for any instructed or permitted malfeasance.

6. In the face of today's complexities—some of which baffle the experts—the average citizen is not going to attain competency fast enough and fully enough to meet the decisions required of him by his freedom. Yet there is plenty of experience to prove he can go a surprisingly long way toward doing so when he gets enough able and honorable help. It is the opportunity and the obligation of responsible thought-leaders both to help the individual get as far as he can go himself—and then to persuade him to accept sound advice from there on—about how he can better attack the obstacles which are preventing him from maximizing his contributions and corresponding rewards as worker, consumer and saver.

7. The most ominous question right now is really not who should do what, but how much time we have left to do it.

Chapter II

THE POLITICAL SOPHISTICATION REQUIREMENT

Our current crisis—over bargaining table and other even more important matters—results from misunderstanding about how we make our living and how we can improve that living.

It is an *economic* and *moral* crisis. But it has to be—and is being—handled as a *political* matter.

This means that—unless our representatives are persuaded there has been a change in what is "good politics" with the public majority—the attempted remedy of the present trouble will only compound the trouble by following further the same faulty ideas which got us into this trouble.

This is because of the hard realities of *political* pressure on representatives. Too many of us credit political institutions with being all wise and all powerful. But even in a dictatorship, the ruler dares not go much beyond what the public majority rightly or wrongly believes at the moment is what should be done.

In our case, we simply cannot expect to go on enjoying the opportunities and rewards we have had—and to go around free to think, speak and act so largely as we please—*unless* a safe majority of us will not only come quickly to *know* what is the right thing to do in the individual and common interest but also *persist in doing* that right thing *voluntarily* no matter what outwardly attractive but essentially evil blandishments are offered to the contrary.

We have to remember that all previous attempts at a free society have failed because of the incompetence and cupidity of those citizens who made up the voting majority and exercised the force of majority public opinion. There is no guarantee ours will not fail for the same reason.

To escape such a fate—and meanwhile just to surmount the current crisis—the majority of us need to meet three requirements for competency in making decisions in our own interest. They are *economic understanding, moral fortitude and political sophistication.*

Where an issue or decision is beyond the capacity of the individual citizen, the citizen must take the advice of a soundly trusted thought leader who is not a politician or who—at least at the moment—is giving genuinely non-partisan advice.

This means that part of any real correction must of course come from the corrected actions of the individuals making up the sovereign majority. But the major and finally determining correction will have to come from the leverage exercised by the agents for the public majority in response to changed instructions or permissions emanating from the majority.

Let's examine in some detail the necessity for the individual constituent to meet his political sophistication requirement.

The average citizen making up the public majority does seem to be beginning to sense that something-for-nothing political promises are not being kept—and that such projects promising the most attractive yield have been the ones failing in the biggest way.

16

Yet the citizen seems deaf to what these experiences are saying to him. For he goes right on doing these two things which are obviously contrary to his interest in an area where he should by now know better, and which thus mean that he is rather carelessly violating his responsibility to himself:

1. If he finally rejects the old promiser, he immediately embraces a new promiser with obviously the same inherent inability to deliver.
2. He goes on assuming he had a "seat in the stands" as an unaffected observer. He knows he did not get the bonanza promised. But he does not think he is out anything—whereas, of course, the cost of the failed attempt was at his expense and is only being hidden from him in the higher prices and fewer job opportunities he is taught to blame on business.

The need is clearly to help such a citizen look with newly seeing eyes at the age-old fact that politicians cannot deliver something-for-nothing, that the costly attempts to *appear* to be doing so are at the expense of the citizen expecting the benefits that do not arrive, and that the fault is not with the politician but with the citizen who will naively elect only the politician who makes what should be recognized as thoroughly ridiculous promises.

He has to be brought face to face with the fact that *he cannot afford to leave politics to the politicians.* He has to do his part in providing not only majority constituency *direction* to insure his representatives staying on the right track but also majority constituency *support* to insure their not being thrown out of office for sticking to the right track.

This requires breaking up a habit of mind—too prevalent even among otherwise savvy people—to the effect that "What we need is to elect a good man with the guts to stand on principle." We have had, and have, lots of good men in office. But no successful politician has "the guts" to do what will militate against his election or re-election.

Most every believer in something-for-something eco-nomics has had the experience of voting for a "good" man and then seeing him act not so good in office. If asked about this, the representative will usually confess in confidence that, as long as there is any chance for a good bill to pass or a bad bill to lose,—either of which is too rare these days—he will stick on the proper side to the end. But when there are very bad bills which can-not be defeated, he will frequently vote for them. His reasoning is he cannot afford to give his opponents any chance to prove he is always against what the misled majority of his constituents are for. Asked if he is not thereby purposely deceiving the voters who trust him, he will in effect say: "Certainly, but it's so important for me to be here that I just have to do what makes that possible." He may embarrassingly add "What do you see as the alternative? What would *you* do?"

So when the citizen allows elected representatives to take over responsibilities involving jobs, prices and free-dom, he had better be prepared for such matters to be handled in about the way the public majority actively insists or negligently assumes they should be handled. The only hope of the citizen is thus to see that he him-self—and all the fellow citizens within the span of his possible influence—are competent and active in guiding and auditing the representatives as to their serving real-ity and not misrepresenting unreality, no matter how seemingly attractive.

In what follows, I make no distinction between the constituents of government representatives and of union representatives. While there may be notable exceptions, majority employee opinion will generally be found to coincide pretty closely with majority public opinion in the surrounding area.

There are many sanctioned uses of the word "political." But its use here throughout will be in *the one narrow sense* of what is bad for, but will look good to, the constituents involved.

I first wrote down the foregoing definition in another connection on a rainy day in camp when on a fishing trip in Canada's Laurentian Mountains. A little worried about it, I looked up the word in the camp's battered old 1857 Webster's Dictionary which had survived the mice for a hundred years. Among the definitions of "political" was this: "Devoted to a scheme rather than a principle." So I feel warranted in the use of the word in the limited way indicated.

The individual represented has the dual duty first of knowing what ought to be done and then of being alert, perceptive, equipped and tough enough to keep his representative properly disciplined and working genuinely in the constituent's interest. Constant vigilance is required to prevent the representative from intentionally or unintentionally working in his own economic and/or political interest to the neglect or exclusion of, or even in direct opposition to, his constituent's interests.

I for one, believe we have much better politicians than most of us deserve. These politicians in government and in unions promise, and try to do in office, what the people who do the electing either *want* done—or will negligently or naively *permit* being done—and *not* what those voters *ought* to want done in their own real interest.

The problem and the process may be illustrated as below—where

B represents the bad—such as a spurious and damaging something-for-nothing quest

G represents the good—such as the honest and rewarding something-for-something course

M represents the voting majority that will come to the polls, or the excisers of majority public opinion between elections.

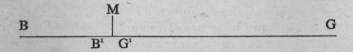

When research discloses that the majority in a particular politician's national, state, local or union constituency is as far over as M, even the best-intentioned candidate does not dare run on a platform that's over at G where his convictions and personal preferences are. If he wants to be elected—and he practically always does (unless he is a Buckley running for Mayor of New York) for that is "the name of the game" in politics—he will dare run no farther toward G, and no farther away from M, than G¹. Likewise the collectivist-leaning candidate—no matter how naively or deceitfully dedicated he may be to the futile something-for-nothing quest—does not dare run at B but makes it abundantly clear that not only what he promises but also *what he claims to believe in* is at B¹.

Thus we have the familiar sight of competing candidates running on platforms which are claimed to be diametrically opposed but are substantially the same—with either as the winner, when later in office, acting just about as his defeated opponent would have.

Hence, what has to be done *first* is to help the public majority move over toward G. This has to be done *between* elections, as there just isn't enough time to do so during a nominating or electing campaign, and anyhow the candidates will not take the chance of running on a platform they are not sure the public majority is *already for* or *tending rapidly toward*.

For, when the public majority has been moved substantially toward G between elections, then this is not only what we see, during campaigns but also what we see *in office meanwhile* as well as later.

In such an improved situation it is to be noted that even the something-for-*nothing* addict is necessarily running on a sounder platform—and will *act more soundly in office*—than would be true of the something-for-*something* motivated candidate when the public majority is less well-informed and less sophisticated politically.

In this connection it needs especially to be kept in mind that it is not necessary to wait for an election to effect a change. Good and bad men do not adjust their positions and action in office just at election time. They move right or left *between elections* just as fast as they hear convincingly from home that their constituency is so moving.

The machinery of politics puts a lag on change wanted or permitted by the electorate. And the vested interest in status-quo ideas and jobs gets more resistant as an institution grows in size. This is theoretically bad, and usually is bad in practice. But sometimes this lag is good, and there are those who believe our government's founding fathers, for instance, purposely built in some of this lag in order to dampen any of the public's hasty desires which may be ill-advised.

21

An important evidence of this is the way so much of our freedom and well-being has survived the something-for-nothing quest of the past 40 years in particular. We are beholden for this to the manner in which the north-south coalition of Republicans and Democrats has had the indispensable aid of conservative committee chairmen whose seigniority derives from long service to "safe" constituencies. We are in bad enough shape as a result of what did get through into law, but this would be a sadly different country—and ours a sadly different life—if any substantial percentage of the other wildly impractical and immoral proposals had gotten past their committees of origin, and then the Rules Committee, and had arrived on the floors of the House and Senate for record voting by representatives afraid that their constituents would not understand if they voted right.

That is, of course, exactly the wrong means toward a good end in a free society—and is a defeat of the democratic process—but we can thank our lucky stars that the mistaken process has yielded as good a result as it has.

So, to repeat, unless the individual citizen making up the majority is sufficiently knowledgeable, sophisticated and vigilant, he will continue too usually to get what is bad for but looks good to him—or which he carelessly or naively assumes is good for him—as a member of that majority which is not living up to its freeman responsibility to take care of its own interest capably.

Probably the most welcome and rewarding "dawn" of political sophistication comes in the form of recognition that "something-for-everybody" politics does not come free from the state or from somebody else but comes not only at the expense of everybody but also at everybody's *intolerably high expense* no matter how hidden from view in the early stages.

It is not enough for some few to become capable.

Politics is a game of numbers—of one man, one vote—of quantity and not quality. So, inescapably, the majority has to become competent, or we are lost as a free and well-to-do people.

Constituents elect and support the biggest promisers who have managed to establish the necessary credibility. The voter's duty to himself is to accord that credibility only after very competently scrutinizing the promises.

By the same token, what a "good" representative needs is primarily a majority which has had its wayward economic ideas constantly corrected, its moral responsibility constantly put back up front, and its political sophistication constantly repaired from the damage done by skillful misleaders. In addition, so far as "guts" are concerned, what he really needs is clear knowledge plus an inspired sense of mission by which—within the relatively narrow limits allowed him as a politcian—to help his constituents keep proofed against outwardly alluring demagogic distractions.

In short, the good or bad done by elective agencies depends on enlightened ethics of the politician. And such enlightened ethics have to be persuasively or forcibly supplied by constituents having equally or even more enlightened ethics.

It must be kept in mind that this is no detached academic or philosophic matter. It is an immediately serious one for everybody—and way beyond any material consideration. For, regardless of the economic, moral and political lessons of history—and despite the protections *theoretically* provided by our laws since long ago—what we fondly regard as our inalienable "rights" hang by the flimsy thread of current public whim. *In practice,* not only do we have no "property" rights—but also no "constitutional" rights, no "inherent" rights, and even no "God-given" rights—except as

23

the public majority is prompted to order or permit their day-to-day continuance.

The most sobering and salutary fact the citizen can keep before him is that *politics—at its rawest and ultimate—is force*.

In the case of a corrupted or even just gullible electorate—under dictatorship and democracy alike—the function of politics becomes largely promising the constituency benefits taken by force from others, then trying to *appear* to be delivering at the expense of others while trying to *hide* the bitter truth that what the constituency is getting is not only at its own expense but at a much higher expense than if the constituency had itself produced—and exchanged voluntarily with each other—what was wanted.

Our only chance to avoid gullibility—and to avoid being corrupted without even knowing it—is to stay free. To stay free—and live well—we must in the majority become sufficiently competent and sufficiently vigilant to guide our representatives properly. The good representatives will gladly follow the guidance. The bad ones will do so out of fear.

Chapter III

THE MORAL REQUIREMENT

But even the most spectacular corrections in political sophistication—and in economic understanding, which will be discussed next—will not remove the problem. These corrections will take us a long way toward doing so, but still not nearly far enough.

There is an inescapable *moral* requirement for our continued freedom and the enjoyment of the rest of the material and non-material well-being open to us.

All through history—and all around the world now—is compelling evidence that man can be free and have a high level of material living only where there is encouragement of the creation and investment of private capital, where there is thus the opportunity for greatly increased output per man through mechanization and specialization, and where the specialists work for each other through the medium of free-market exchange.

Somebody has said "there is a little larceny in everyone". And the best of us would probably steal a little food if we or our family were really starving. But too many of us from all racial origins and at every economic and educational level—though far removed from starvation—are rationalizing *continuous* thievery as simply the recovery of what has been previously withheld or even stolen from us.

Too many assume the old rules just do not apply any more. We see "theft without guilt" quoted as a new ideology of the young. We see stealing from business regarded not only as more moral than working for business but also as a "justified re-distribution of wealth."

Entirely too many of us are trying to have our politicians conduct "organized free-loading" for us. Too many are subscribing to the fallacious and immoral idea that individual or organized *force*—and not *worth* in willing exchange—is the way to get what is wanted from the other fellow. This idea has only to be followed to its conclusion—where nobody is producing and everybody is trying to take—until there not only *is* nothing to take but, of course, *should* be nothing.

Not even freedom can stand this. Freedom, private property and the moral order go inseparably hand in hand. A free society has to be morally based. And any society condoning thievery is bound to fail.

We owe our state of freedom and well-being to the confidence we citizens have had that our fellow citizens, in the vast majority, are not going to steal from us, or destroy our exposed property, or take away our output and savings by gang force, but are going to repay loans and trade with us on what they and we regard as a something-for-*something* exchange basis.

There are signs that we may be losing this confidence. We had better start deserving to get it back.

Examples are all too plentiful along the lines of these two random ones: An FBI report says shoplifting is growing at the rate of 20% a year. Retail store shrinkage—which includes shoplifting, employee theft, careless sales slip and bookkeeping errors, and merchandise spoiled through negligence—currently runs about $3.5 billion annually. All of this means that—

along with highjacking and payments extracted for so-called "protection"—retail prices consumers pay even for food and clothing are 5 to 7% higher in too many communities than they otherwise would be. Shoplifting at Atlanta's Emory University Campus book store is reportedly running $15,000 per year.

If religion is not inspiring us sufficiently—and if other influences at home, at school, at church and in the market places are failing to keep us wanting to do right for right's sake—then we as a people, for very selfish practical reasons, had better readopt the old principle that "honesty is the best policy".

This may sound to some as futile wishful thinking in the face of today's predatory urge here and around the world. Nevertheless, we had better work to make this come true, or we will be the sad losers of the freedom and well-being that have set us apart from all others elsewhere through all time.

Chapter IV

THE ECONOMIC COMPETENCY REQUIREMENT

The economic competency requirement will be the hardest to meet for most citizens either directly or through their thought-leaders. There is so much to do and undo.

I, for one, believe the essence of the problem is in our false expectations grown now to heroic proportions.

The wide misunderstanding of inflation, unemployment, productivity and profit—highlighted now at the bargaining table and elsewhere—testifies to how the public majority at all levels has been misled by its own wishful thinking, by the teachings of its most trusted advisers, and by the silence of most businessmen.

The public's conspicuous confusion over these four presently so troublesome issues is only one important surfacing of a much deeper misunderstanding. All of us are freshly impatient to live a whole lot better right away. That is understandable—and we *can* readily do so, provided each citizen will really see and do his obligated part toward that end.

But hard to understand—after all our much vaunted education at home, at school, and at church—is that most of our fellow citizens so clearly demand and expect that their take will be much greater than their contribution. They seem to want too much too soon for too little in return . . . . and thus want "instant utopia" too largely from someone else. For there is the foolish belief that government, or private business, or future generations can and will somehow supply the difference now between what these citizens produce and what they want.

Such unreal economic expectations—involving such distressing moral aberrations—are rooted mainly, I believe, in these three causes:

1. The majority does not realize that consumers pay most all the expenses of any business which long survives, and that any exceptions are relatively unimportant; that these expenses—including all wages and taxes—are paid in current prices, or in delayed progress in future values, or in both; and that most always even a strike over wages is not a conflict of interest between workers and owners but between workers and consumers among which latter are, of course, the workers themselves.

2. The majority does not know that *individual* citizens, as tax-paying consumers, supply all the money government spends, regardless of whether this money is taken from consumers in direct taxes, or in the taxes government levies on business and then has business collect from consumers in prices, or in the tax of inflation arising from government's borrowing and then deceitfully counterfeiting under the pleasant name of "monetizing debt."

3. The majority does not recognize the obvious fact that we can and do have only what we pro-

duce; that the level of living can be raised only by us, as specialists, doing more for each other; that it is naive as well as dishonest for the majority to go on putting its present heavy dependence on the economically pitiful and morally disgraceful idea of getting something-for-nothing *for the many* through gang force imposed on some *few* via the voting booth, the bargaining table, or privileged violence; and that even the new "Quality of Life"—which is now so eagerly sought by so many of the young in particular—will, if it comes, *not* come free but will take a lot of work by a lot of people who will have been forced or persuaded to support all the others who expect to enjoy this relaxed and responsibility-escaped life. While non-productive of the goods and services they will still demand, the exponents of this sort of life-to-be seem to believe that what they want will continue to come to them through some effortless and unrewarded working of "the economy."

I sincerely believe the dire consequences of the majority following these false ideas are largely what we see all round us now not only in our inflation, unemployment, restricted productivity, and debilitated profits, but also in our problems of privileged violence, law defiance, police corruption, welfare abuses, drug addiction, high absenteeism and turnover, poor quality, indifferent and impolite service, scorn for rewards being based on worth, rejection of the principle of individual responsibility, and perhaps the worst of our race and campus outbreaks, along with what may be the beginnings of opposition to our keeping militarily strong enough to insure that our country's security will be inviolate in this still very bad world.

Let's look at these four areas where we in the public majority seem to need in our own interest to correct our own ideas and practices and see that our representatives correct theirs:

1. Inflation

The key area where the public majority most needs to correct its absurdly false expectations—and thereby know how to stop doing damage to itself while presuming just the opposite—is in the realm of who and what causes inflation, who can stop it, and who meanwhile inescapably and justly pays the bill for the wrong course being taken.

Inflation is not caused by war, or by business greed, or by the government supplying those services for which the public is willing to pay. Inflation comes only from government being forced or allowed by its citizens to create worthless extra money (and credit) where there are no extra goods and services to match. Our government has been doing this because our representatives sense the political necessity of at least *appearing* to meet the following dual requirement put on them by the public majority that does not for one moment suspect this is what it is doing.

1. To provide the money for the government to pay for those goods and services which the public majority wants or permits some or all of the public to receive at so-called "government expense". The big increase here is due to home-sector spending and not to Vietnam.

   The public majority loosely assumes the money for this is going to come from somewhere else, and would itself flatly refuse to pay the cost visibly or knowingly. Our government—believing it politically necessary to at least appear to be doing what its constituents demand or allow—is thus driven by the public to resort to the deceitful process of collecting the cost from that same unsuspecting public through the tax of inflation hidden in higher consumer prices.

2. To pump out added worthless cash to increase the number and cut the value of all our dollars, so that consumers will have enough cheapened dollars to buy at the higher consumer prices now necessitated by the total of the artificially higher pay—that is, the total of the higher wages, benefits and higher cost-of-living allowances. This higher total imposed in the absence of higher output to match, will only kill or reduce jobs if money is left at its old value, and is in accordance with the pay practices demanded or permitted by the affected but unseeing consuming public itself.

Thus what government is really doing here is, first, to promote or sanction the unworkable pay increase and then promptly wipe out the expected added buying power of that increase in an attempt to mask or to delay temporarily the job-killing effect of such pay raises unmatched by raised output. This restores the wage-price relationship existing prior to the now worthless wage increase. It is important to note that unearned pay increases—forced above what the free market would yield—are *not inflationary in themselves* but *do become inflationary* when they lead government to cheapen the value of money correspondingly.

The resulting inflation from both 1 and 2 above shows up as a consumer tax. It is the most brutal, the most debilitating, and the most deceitful of all taxes. It ensues from the consumers' own action or negligence, or both, and cannot be escaped by consumers. Employers cannot save their employees from it. Once in the system, government has no power to prevent it from being finally collected from the consumer. Inflation can be arrested only by heading it off at the source.

Thus, to stop inflation, the total of both No. 1 and No. 2 above must be tapered down to at most 3% a year for the country as a whole (to match the presumed or hope-for productivity increase.) This means, of course, that only part of the job would have been accomplished if our government should succeed in stopping the inflation (of the No. 2 kind above) which is triggered by employment cost increases unmatched by increased production of goods and services. The other part would go undone—and inflation would continue on up—if our government continued to believe it "good politics" to keep stepping up, as it is now, the deficit spending to cover the added things it is "giving" the public which may or may not want them but which at any rate fondly believes it is escaping paying for them.

The $40 billion deficit still expected this year even in the face of efforts at dampening the excessive wages—not to mention the $100 billion deficit now being seriously discussed—is far beyond anything that could possibly do its intended "stimulating" of the economy sufficiently, and will almost surely show up in both more inflation and more unemployment. In fact, just as the worn out dope addict finally ceases to respond to even the progressively bigger shots because his body is too jaded or debilitated to have any reserve to summon up, so our economic system must eventually fail to respond. There is some suspicion that we may be now nearing that stage. And meanwhile, all this deficit spending is going into the tax of inflation to be paid in consumer prices.

The majority needs to know that a rise in the cost-of-living is simply the natural market forces collecting back the worthless extra money for which there are no matching goods. If such extra money—thus collected from consumers as *the tax of inflation*— is then *refunded* to them in a cost-of-living adjustment, the inflationary process (of extra money with no extra goods to match) begins all over again. But this time it starts from a new higher base with its still more damaging effect in prices. This pyramiding only has to be kept up to have us suffer here the kind of disastrous unemployment or inflation—or both—we have seen elsewhere but have fondly thought could not happen to us.

The majority needs to know what really happens when a settlement—on supposedly an "ability-to-pay" basis—is imposed on some one employer who leads in size and profit conspicuously enough to be a pattern setter. Such settlement will raise prices or unemployment, or both, across most all business—simply because, once imposed on the pattern-setter, the "ability to pay" idea will be dropped and the settlement will be heralded as setting the new market price pattern all must pay regardless of so-called "ability-to-pay." And the public must be helped to know that the cost of such settlement will show up not only in the cost of *wages* but also in the cost of *purchases and other services* for the pattern-setter and for most other *employers*.

The hottest question right now is why prices are wiping out these something-for-nothing wage gains so much

35

faster than they did a little while back. The answer is that these successively higher inflation binges are so akin to taking dope—for a long time each new higher level of shots makes us feel good in the beginning, but this is inevitably followed by the proportionally higher agony of the after-effects. We started a new wave of inflation in the early 1960's. We felt good for a while because the new higher costs were still mixed with some old costs along the goods-in-process pipeline, and the full effect of the newly inflated money was not yet getting into end-product costs and consumer prices. But these costs are now showing up with the rush which is so suddenly skyrocketing the cost of living.

Employee compensation accounts for 75% to 85% of total cost from raw material to finished goods, and any idea that 10% to 20% yearly increase in cost in this area can be offset by only what can be done in the other 15% to 25% area seems obviously unrealistic in the extreme. If the value of money should be kept constant—while these synthetic wage increases go on up—the increasing cost cannot be met out of the prices consumers can and will pay in old dollars. So any effort at stabilizing the value of money is bound to fail—unless money wages are also stabilized. Such stabilization cannot come by unions *forcing* wages up or by government *forcing* them down. It must come voluntarily from the parties—under the discipline of a public majority which knows it is paying the whole bill—or we are lost as even a reasonably free people.

The majority needs to understand—and to keep firmly in mind in the days ahead—the reason for the spectacular failure of the government's brief effort to stabilize the value of the consumer's dollar by trying only to balance the budget, to restrict credit expansion, and thus to stop the manufacture of worthless extra money for which there was no matching output. The public was not told by the government—or by enough others of us to be effective—that this effort was bound to fail if unmatched money wages were to go on up arbitrarily.

We are now (April 1972) in "Phase II". The majority needs help, as never before, in getting wise not only to the current futility—but also to the long term damage to worker and consumer—of attempted controls over a sovereign public which does not understand the causes of the trouble and which, as each unsound measure fails, will demand the cure be sought in still more of the same unsound controls.

The long and sad history of pay and price controls is that they have always, in peace and war, not only failed of their purpose but also caused just the opposite of the results intended. I have scar tissue all over me from having had to try to help make them work in World War II.

As long as government and non-government controllers have to be responsive to a misled public majority, wage *rates* will be unwisely favored while prices and profits will be destructively squeezed to the damage not only of the current and future values attainable but also of the number of jobs and the *real* wages earned in those jobs.

For instance, profits obviously cannot absorb the higher costs of recent pay increases already accumulating in the goods-in-process pipe line and soon to show up in finished goods costs, and they cannot absorb future periodic wage increases or the adjustment of "inequities" which play such a characteristic part in any control period. If wage rates should be stabilized as of a given date, cost increases from the prior wage increases will continue for some time thereafter to show up in consumer prices or lost jobs or both. Thus it is unrealistic

37

to try to level off wages and prices as of the same date.

The past results—which can be expected to be duplicated in any such further effort now—were that the politically necessary price and profit squeeze works to:

disrupt and reduce output of the very goods most wanted and needed by lower-income citizens,

promote our black markets and force lawbreaking by most all our best people,

lower the level of living, and

leave the public more wrathful than ever as to the still wrongly suspected causes of the trouble and, as indicated, more likely to demand or support still more destructive measures in the belief they are remedies.

The only solution to this pay and price problem in even a reasonably free society is for the public majority not only to know the facts directly (or take the guidance of thought-leaders worth trusting) but also to be so sophisticated as to be open to no nonsense. The stabilization of pay and prices—around attractive values actually attainable—cannot come from union, business or government force. It can only come *voluntarily* in a something-for-something market under the watchful eye of an alerted, informed and politically sophisticated public majority. The greatest good that can come out of "The Freeze" and "Phase II" is to alert citizens and their thought-leaders to this necessity.

As one important aid to this, the public majority needs to keep up a sophisticated alert to the unlovely fact that inflation *purposely* taxes citizens in a way most citizens will not suspect and for uses they would never permit if *they* knew *they* were footing the bill. This is in accordance with the ancient adage that "the ideal tax is the one that gets the most feathers out of the goose with the least squawk."

Inflation is a regressive tax of the first order. For the farther down the earning and saving scale the particular citizen is, the heavier is the relative impact of this tax on him.

Such a deceitful course is forced on government officals by that majority of us who will not elect or re-elect them if they directly and visibly tax us for enough to cover all the expenditures we insist government make. Our inflation is thus due to our representatives *trying to appear to be making good* on what are our futile and unworthy expectations of something-for-nothing. Thus, under Democrats and Republicans alike, we force our government to run a counterfeit money machine with the same fraudulent intent and result that would get the individual counterfeiter put right in jail.

These inflationary forces and results do not, of course, proceed in exact mathematical lockstep. Habit of mind, varying confidence, reserves on consumer shelves, lower-cost ingredients still in the pipeline, the different times at which various segments of the population get the added worthless money, and temporary shifts in productivity and in monetary policy—any or all of these contribute to delays or surges in the pace at which new inflation gets into consumer prices. Intended here is only a broad indication, and there has been necessarily some oversimplification. What I have been trying to do is simply to illustrate that it *is* possible for the non-economist among us, such as myself, to offer some *beginning* information that will help our fellow citizens reject the wrong ideas and actions with which they are now harming themselves in this inflation area. For inflation can, *in the end,* be arrested only by an informed and sophisticated public majority understanding the direct and indirect causes of inflation so that it will see that both its own actions and those of its representatives head off inflation at the source.

In short and to repeat, the public majority is itself inescapably responsible for our inflation, and only that majority can get it stopped.

As a reminder, it is assumed here that the employee majority and the consumer majority are of substantially the same mind as the overall majority.

2. Unemployment

The failure of artificially high wage rates and inflationary government deficits to produce the promised full employment has been very disillusioning to those sponsoring this kind of something-for-nothing quest.

If this failure of false expectations to materialize is as surprising as it is distressing, the public majority needs to understand that where a citizen wants work on a something-for-something basis and is not getting it, the reason is almost always that his services are not worth what they would cost *the ultimate consumer* from whom the bill has to be collected in the end and who is the sole final judge of the worth involved.

The price may be greater than the worth to the potential buyer for one or more of several reasons. The typical buyer has been estimated to work only about one hour a day to meet his *basic* needs of food purely for sustenance, clothing purely for covering, and housing purely for shelter. He is estimated to work the other seven hours a day for luxuries in the form of extra satisfactions derived not only from form, color, taste, aroma, comfort, convenience, distinction and other emotional or esthetic attributes but also from the dignity, manners, and pleasant atmosphere involved in the very making of the purchase.

Thus—with the exception of sustenance food not in his freezer—he can put off for quite a while most any purchase, including such important ones as clothes, shoes, tires, cars, appliances, house maintenance, cosmetics, liquor, recreation, etc.

He may be working part time or be unemployed or be on relief—or his savings may be low—and the purchase in question may not yet be high enough up his priority list. He may have ample funds but think the price too high and want to check competitive features and prices or just wait. He may not even want the product at all, preferring one of another industry—may, for instance, decide against a car and for a motorcycle or even a bicycle.

Contrary to usual habit, he may be holding on to his high and rising savings—while using up his inventory or just doing without—because he has lost confidence in what is ahead in sales and jobs and thus fears he had better make more than ordinary provision for what seems an increasingly probable rainy day.

Of the foregoing causes of fewer sales and jobs, the last mentioned is at this writing the most distressing as well as the most disappointing. The hoped-for upturn has refused to materialize seemingly because so many buyers able to buy the normally expected quantity of both producer goods and consumer goods just do not have the confidence to do so.

An added new and unfamiliar cause of unemployment is the growing efficiency and capacity of our foreign competitors. They are killing our jobs through the more attractive values they are supplying to our home market as well as to our former or potential customers abroad. Here are some instances:

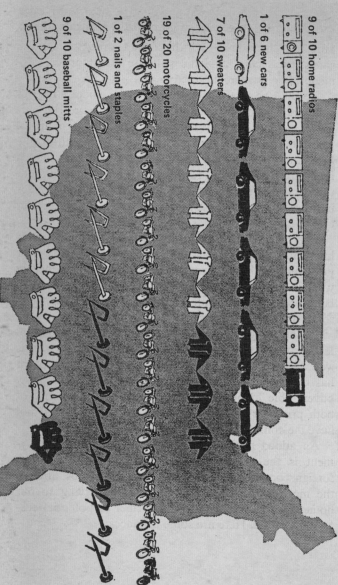

Foreign products now account for . . . .

9 of 10 home radios

1 of 6 new cars

7 of 10 sweaters

19 of 20 motorcycles

1 of 2 nails and staples

9 of 10 baseball mitts

The cause of our losing out is in our wage rates and our productivity, as so graphically illustrated here:

 IS THERE STILL TIME?

Our challenge: Can productivity bridge the gap?

COUNTRY	1970 HOURLY LABOR COSTS	GAP	% MORE U.S. PAYS
U.S.	$4.18	-0-	-0-
West Germany	2.27	$1.91	84
France	1.82	2.36	130
Italy	1.73	2.45	142
Great Britain	1.60	2.58	161
Japan	0.95	3.23	340

Estimated by INDUSTRY WEEK; includes fringes and benefits.

Quoted from Industry Week

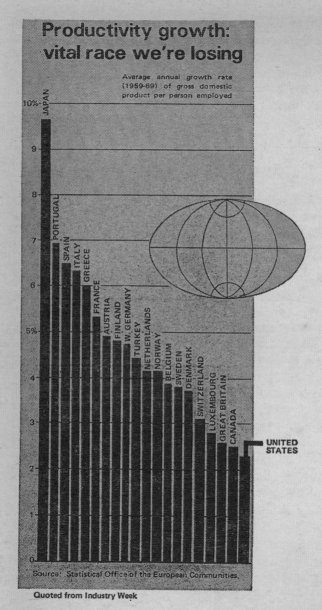

Productivity growth: vital race we're losing

Average annual growth rate (1959-69) of gross domestic product per person employed

Source: Statistical Office of the European Communities.

Quoted from Industry Week

44

All this is suddenly very embarrassing and depressing. We are used to being first, not second or third. We are accustomed to being on the upgrade, not the downgrade.

And it is also very disillusioning and disappointing. For a long time we seemed to be successfully turning back the hard laws of something-for-something economics. Our growing volume of sales and jobs masked the way we were missing our opportunity, squandering our advantage and building up the trouble we now face.

For decades our consumers had been enabling our businesses to pay much higher wages than those elsewhere, to work shorter hours, to provide savings, pensions and social security obligations, to pass on most all the cost of strikes, featherbedding, productivity opposition and other needless subtractions from values otherwise possible, and yet keep production and sales ahead of any foreign competition.

We could do this because of a variety of concurrent causes. Our volume of manufactured goods had kept way ahead of that of all other nations because of our rapid invention of attractive new consumer goods, our mounting investment in large specialized facilities to mass-produce the new volume ever more economically, our growing population able to buy the new production, and our exchange of finished goods for raw materials with foreigners who did not yet have the technology, facilities and volume to enable them to meet their own slowly developing markets much less compete with us here at home. For a good part of this period, we also were on the make, were on the rise, and had the competitive spirit. We had confidence in ourselves, and we went about our destiny with enthusiasm. We believed ourselves winners whom no one could ever successfully challenge.

However, due to our well-intended but naive generosity abroad—and to our being so wasteful of natural resources and so unrealistic as to pay and productivity practices here at home—our foreign competitors have now managed to catch up with us in technology, in quality, in the capacity and efficiency of their facilities, and in the confidence and energy going into their competitive spirit, while their costs of both labor and government remain far below ours.

They now match our volume in many important lines, and have already put us out of business in some. We are now importing both raw materials and finished goods which we formerly exported. In short, where we formerly had the advantage, we are now increasingly at a disadvantage.

Japan and Germany continue to get farther ahead of us by investing faster than we in improved technology and facilities for economic volume. Yet as long as they and others even match our technology and volume—while their employee productivity is so high and pay so low—jobs here will be fewer because of the resulting preferred position which the foreign producers enjoy in our own former markets both here and abroad.

Some foreign governments add to our production cost disadvantage by excusing taxes on exports to us and adding tariffs and other penalties on imports from us. This means that we are competing with a real wage that is even lower than the figures indicate, since both the subsidies on exports and duties on imports have to be collected back from the citizens of the foreign country in direct or hidden taxes. And our trying to match the machinations of these foreign governments might temporarily make certain lines somewhat more competitive in foreign markets but would add to our domestic taxes, our cost of living, and soon, if not immediately, to our unemployment.

Likewise, our use of high tariffs or other import barriers—to protect our higher-cost products from foreign competition in our home markets—would raise the cost of living, cut real wages, and kill jobs both through poorer value and through preventing foreigners from earning the dollars with which to buy those of our products otherwise still saleable to them. There is, in the end, just no way to compete *with* a low-cost producer but *to be* a low-cost producer.

Another influence contributing to unemployment is our welfare system. Millions of citizens now on welfare do not belong there. Much of both the incentive and the possibility of their getting and holding a job have been eliminated by bad laws and by those laws being administered in ways even worse than intended. There is the inevitable political corruption and other gigantic waste in handling the huge sums through political appointees.

All this needless extra cost has to be added to the direct taxes, or to the consumer prices, *or to both,* which those citizens *not* on welfare have to pay. It reduces the buying power for—and hence *reduces the jobs available on*—products and services which could otherwise absorb some of the unemployed.

The public majority needs to preceive that it is not "government" money—but consumer dollars and jobs —which are being squandered not only on those citizens unwarrantedly on welfare but also on the corruption and other waste in the administration of the system. It will not be politically possible even to begin to clean up the scandalous welfare mess until the individual members of the public majority begin to pay proper attention to the hard fact that it is *their* money and jobs they see being wasted locally and nationally in the welfare area.

Most of us are probably the worst fooled by minimum wage laws and what they do to employment as well as inflation. They seem so fair and so innocent of any bad results of real consequence.

The first effect of such laws is to price out of the market so many present and prospective workers who are precisely those whom the laws are wrongly presumed to help—such, for instance, as the blacks, the youth and other unskilled whom the rest of us, who are still employed, then have to support in idleness.

The second effect of these so-called minimum wage laws is to raise all the other rates which are above the minimum. Once these lower rates are arbitrarily raised, the formerly ruling differentials between the various skills are promptly reestablished progressively from the bottom clear up to the top through either market or union action. This process is vividly reported by The State Labor News of Columbus, Ohio, in its September 25, 1971 issue thus:

"MINIMUM WAGE INCREASES MEANS MAXIMUM WAGE INCREASES"

"Every indication points to enactment of a minimum wage increase in this session of Congress. Both President Nixon and Congress agree on an increase in the present minimum wage rate.

"The only difference between Congress and the President is a matter of timing. Congress wants an increase from $1.60 an hour to $2.00 to go into effect this year. The President wants the increase extended over a two, three year period, with $1.80 an hour this year, increased to $2.00 an hour in 1973.

"This minimum wage increase is a favorite organized labor issue, that in labor union lexion has no limit. Already you hear in labor union circles that the $2.00 an hour rate is too low and should be increased to $2.50 an hour.

"Organized labor goes on the premises, that if you want to increase the maximum wage rate, you must increase the minimum. Usually the formula calls for a 4 to 1 ratio of minimum to maximum.

"Organized labor is looking to the next heavy round of wage increases in 1973 and 1974. An increase in the *minimum* wage rate in 1971 means an increase in *maximum* wage rates in 1973-74."

Just as the government prices jobs out of the market by this arbitrary minimum wage process with the public majority's support or tolerance, so do union imposed increases—above the market and unmatched by added output—likewise trigger inflation and unemployment at the expense of the very public which actively or passively authorizes those increases.

We of the majority need to get the vivid picture of how this setting pay artificially above the market also forces employers to eliminate jobs through increasing their investment in technology much faster than is economic for the public—and this on top of the public being also saddled with having to support the displaced in idleness. For instance, a fairly typical case would be where an employer is forced to contract for an increase of pay and benefits rate by roughly 5% a year to 25% over the five year term. In those five years, the company's prices, volume, roughly 6% profit, and *total payroll cost* could remain relatively constant—but the *number of employees* at the end would have to be 25% fewer than at the beginning. The company management would obviously have had to scurry around to develop technological improvements in which it could rewardingly invest in elimnatng 5% of the jobs each year in order to stay alive and, in the process, to be able to sell goods that would provide employment to protect the other 75% of jobs at the end of five years.

49

In short, the public majority's employment policy—as implemented by the public's representatives and negligently accepted by the majority of us—is forcing employers to keep limiting their employment to those farther and farther up the skill and productivity scale just as fast as the services of the lower producers are progressively priced beyond what consumers will refund to the employers.

Past history and the current world are full of compelling evidence that trying to have pay be more than the worth of the work to the ultimate buyer of the service is inevitably a job-killing process—regardless of whether or not inflation is used to try to mask what is going on.

Thus, the public majority needs to abandon wishful thinking, reject something-for-nothing proposals, and face the hard fact that—if unemployment is to be minimized while still preserving reasonably free choice in the market—a way must be found to restore our ability to offer values sufficiently attractive to the willing buyer here and abroad.

It will be a miracle if such a way can be found other than in doing *all four* of the following:

1. Create the needed new savings—and encourage their investment in arm-lengthening designs and equipment—*faster now than foreign competitors do*. This is the exact opposite of what we are now doing.
2. Raise sharply the output from the inner resources of employees through full skill, care, and effort, accompanied by the elimination of featherbedding and other waste and by the rejuvenation of cooperation toward all possible improvements in the values that can be offered customers here and abroad.
3. Cut out the needless waste of government—

and pare down even those government services which are really desired but of lower priority— in order to reduce the cost of government that inescapably raises the prices which have to be charged buyers here and abroad.

4. Sharply reduce the gap between our pay rates and those of Germany and Japan in particular. While rates abroad have recently been going up faster than ours *in percentage,* their base is so low that *in dollar* increases we thus far continue way ahead, and these dollar increases have to be added to rates which are already way out of line and thereby become more so.

All four are going to be bitterly hard to come by— emotionally as well as economically. But we have no other choice if we want to regain the high road of real wage increases. These can come only through productivity increases.

3. Productivity

Too many of us seem unaware of the obvious fact that we can have only what we produce. The accompanying chart is an eloquent message that our level of living goes up as our productivity goes up.

The public majority needs to know just who benefits from gains, and suffers from drops, in that productivity which results from investment in arm-lengthening equipment coupled with the application of skill, care and effort.

To be sure, productivity increases can come from any or all of these three sources:

Owners—through new investment not only of *money*

51

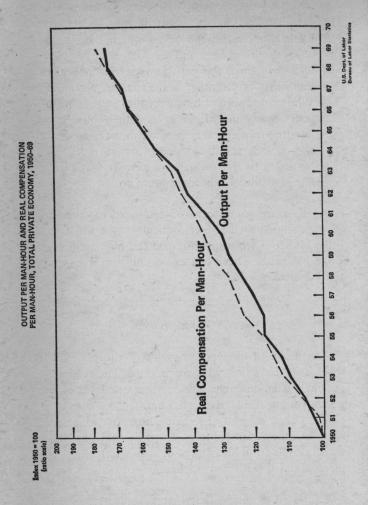

OUTPUT PER MAN-HOUR AND REAL COMPENSATION
PER MAN-HOUR, TOTAL PRIVATE ECONOMY, 1950-69

Index 1950 = 100
(ratio scale)

Real Compensation Per Man-Hour

Output Per Man-Hour

U.S. Dept. of Labor
Bureau of Labor Statistics

52

in arm-lengthening physical facilities but also of *managerial progress* in arm-lengthening ideas, methods, rearrangements, quality and handling of materials, and wisdom and clarity of direction.

Employees—through their *own inner resources* being applied to fuller skill, care and effort.

Customers—through the mix, size and steadiness of their purchases in response to the values offered.

These can be working in the same or conflicting directions at any one time. Some of the influences are evident. Some are practically impossible to perceive in exact quantitative terms at the time—such as in the product mix and managerial areas where the changes tend to occur gradually and constantly.

Incidentally, this inability satisfactorily to separate out the sources and determine the sizes of these various changes as they occur—and especially to separate the other contributions from those on which added pay is to be made to employees for the added output from their inner resources—is what has made collective bargaining based on productivity prove to be generally so frustrating and unworkable.

But for our purposes here, what the public majority now particularly needs help in understanding is that the currently high prices would be a whole lot higher if it had not been for the productivity gains accomplished meanwhile by the steadily increasing investment in these arm-lengthening improvements by private business competing for profit. Prices in the past have not gone up nearly as much as wages, due to such labor-saving gains having *more* than offset the losses from shorter time worked, higher absenteeism and turnover, increased spoilage and lessened application on the job.

Right now in April, 1972, too many feel that prices are rising faster than pay. But they are wrong.

Ever since July, 1971 the month before the freeze— average non-farm pay rates have increased twice as fast as consumer prices. Retail wages have gone up 2½ times as fast, manufacturing pay rates three times as fast, and contract construction wages (even from their high base) about three times as fast as the consumer price index.

In fact, with the exception of some war months, wage rates have risen about twice as fast as prices in every year of this entire century. The difference has, of course, been made up by productivity increases resulting somewhat from increased skill, care and effort but mostly from increased investment in improved facilities.

The basic reason so many of us are misled about this is three fold. First, except for a short period around 1952 or 1953, our government has neglected to show both the wage and price change in the same monthly release. Second, the press and broadcasters have failed to dig up the related wage change to include with their reports of price change. Third, those with a political interest in creating a false impression have thus been given a free hand to mislead.

Perhaps contributing to the ease of our being misled is that most of us tend to lose sight of the size of our annual or other pay rise and are thus disproportionately distressed at seeming always to find each successive purchase priced higher than the last.

But prices are not actually going up as fast as wages even now. And this is all the more remarkable because —whenever an effort is made suddenly to stabilize wages and prices—there is inevitably a lot of recent wage increases which have already been paid but are still back up the pipe line. They have already gone into the costs of raw materials and goods in process but will not show up until later in the costs and prices of finished goods.

We may not have all we want—and we may not be progressing toward that as fast as we would like—but it is not because prices are outstripping wage rates. Our basic problem about living better is how to get more productivity.

As long as these productivity gains were 2% to 3% a year while wages were being forced up 3 to 4%, the difference going into inflation was more or less tolerable. But recent pay increases have been running two to four times any productivity increase, and the whole difference has had to go into higher unemployment, or higher prices, or—as we see—too much of both.

Contrary to what is being fashionably taught and assumed, all real progress comes from some temporary self-denial in order to be able to invest toward the hoped-for later enjoyment of larger and more rewarding benefits. This is what we do when we go to school, protect our health, develop a reputable character, and save some money for the rainy day or brighter satisfactions.

Progress in real wages and real value can likewise come only from *investment* in more productive physical facilities and in fuller human skill, care and effort. Gains in real income—as opposed to worthless pay increases in cheapened dollars which will not buy more—can result only from working harder or more efficiently, saving more, investing more and, as interdependent specialists, producing more per person per year for each other.

The key to sufficient investment in improved facilities —to enable them to do their part in improving productivity and real values—is in a climate of public opinion that endorses and encourages the earning of profits adequate to supply both the ability to save and the incentive to invest.

The key then to having these improved facilities live up to their full potential for goods is the unalterable conviction of all concerned that they should all cooperate fully toward that end—realizing that our real wage can go up only as productivity goes up.

I hope every reader will not only master the accompanying productivity chart (P. 52) and store it in memory for instant recall but will also get copies to give every associate and every other friend, relative and neighbor with the exhortation to spread the story it so eloquently tells. I know of no couple of lines which so debunk the false expectations of something for nothing through higher wages unmatched by higher output.

The most preposterous of the various impractical dreams abounding now must be the one that we can slip gear between incomes and the worth of what we do—"the unshackling of men from the bonds of unfulfilling labor"—and free us all to go around being as unproductive as we please, while at the same time naively demanding of "society" or "the economy" an ever increasing amount and attractiveness of goods and services which would have to be produced by millions of citizens through work not just unfulfilling but often hard, dirty and frustrating. The drafting of the citizens to do the productive work would have to be done by a military backed dictator. And the proven inefficiencies of the planner-directed as compared with the market-directed economy would insure practically every adult having soon to be at productive work—unfulfilling or not—and having a very low level of living in return.

In short, our present foregin competition can be overcome—and our inflation and unemployment can be cured—only as we each succeed in producing more attractive values to exchange with others as willing buyers and sellers in a free market.

56

As already indicated, this increased productivity can come primarily from just two sources: First, from increased investment in arm-lengthening ideas and equipment. Second, from making full use of skill, care and effort.

To come by the required investment, we must get to understand the private business process well enough to appreciate how we simply must see that people have a favorable economic, moral and political climate for the creation and investment of savings. To get the application of the required skill, care and effort, we must again understand private business well enough to appreciate that we are inescapably on a something-for-something basis and that, if we expect to get what we want, we simply have to offer in return an equal value judged from the other fellow's standpoint.

But increased productivity *per man hour* will not solve inflation and give us a higher level of living—if we let the drain from fewer hours worked and from taking care of non-productive citizens increase faster than the output of the citizens still producing. Our level of living is determined by the *output per year* spread over *each man, woman and child* in our country.

Meanwhile, we need to keep in mind the difficulty in meeting even the 3% productivity improvement goal set by the Administration for Phase II. This difficulty is due—in addition to the other familiar causes—to the now rapidly growing proportion of the work force which is in services where the opportunity for investment in arm-lengthening equipment is usually far less than in manufacturing, for instance.

The need for increased productivity in the public interest now takes on a whole new dimension over and beyond the familiar but unmet need of the recent past. This is because for a long time while we were raising our level of living, we were happy to welcome the smokestacks, stream pollution, junk piles, scattered waste, rapid exhaustion of resources, and other damage to the environment which our heedless actions caused.

But workers in both producer and consumer goods and services must now provide enough not only for their own living but also for that of a vast new army of workers who will not be immediately productive for increased home consumption because they will be required:

1. To clean up the waste, remove the pollution, and repair the other damage to the environment.
2. To do the extra work in producing the higher cost ingredients to replace those of easier extraction which we have been exhausting.
3. To produce the finished goods we must trade abroad for the higher cost raw material which we will have to import to replace those formerly available here at much lower cost

How much higher our productivity must be to meet our new operating standards here—and still be able to compete with and sell to foreigners—is vividly illustrated by Brazil's invitation to "come on down and pollute." They would like some of our jobs and former level of both living and polluting.

We all have to keep clearly in mind that the investment and work put into these new activities is at the expense of an equal value in current producer and consumer goods and services. If we do not increase productivity by an equal amount, we will suffer a fall in our level of living.

4. Profit

Profit is even the poor man's best friend. It is the benefactor of all the public. It is the necessary foundation not only for private property and freedom itself but for the rest of our superior material and non-material well-being.

Yet, I hardly need to emphasize the suspicion and hostility on the part of the public majority toward private enterprise and the mechanisms which animate it—such as not only the profit motive but also the competition, the rewards based on worth, and the market as the director of production and distribution of goods and services.

Given this public attitude, it is no wonder that politicians in unions and in government can not only treat businessmen and their recommendations so contemptuously but also find it politically so rewarding to use profit as their favorite whipping boy.

But in profit lies our hope for most of the increased productivity needed to accomplish the more attractive values our situation now demands.

The public majority needs to make certain not only that earned profit on present investments is permitted restoration to a rewarding level, but also that provident citizens are supplied a climate which makes possible both the ability and willingness to save and risk the further funds required for the greatly improved operations.

The imperfections of this system and the misdeeds of the misdoers are very real. But I submit that they are magnified and dwelt upon out of all proportion to the actual benefits produced and to the percentage of its practitioners who do their work honestly and commendably.

What has happened is that business credibility with the public majority—as to results, procedures and even intentions—has been allowed to sink so low that the enemies of our business system find it little or no trouble to have people believe even any slightest slip in a product or service is the intended rule rather than the isolated exception inevitable in human affairs despite the best of intentions.

Obviously, the majority of us must insist that business does correct anything that ought to be corrected in the public interest—including, incidentally, those wrong things which business is now pressured into doing because of the dictates or permits of the majority of us carried out through our representatives.

And businessmen up and down the line simply must learn and do the marketing and repairing of the incentives, practices and rewards of the business sytsem to the same fine degree they do the marketing and repairing of their products and services. This is a forced-draft, catch-up job of no mean proportions, because they have not heretofore been regularly taught this by their predecessors, or by their current superiors, or by their trade press, or by their professional consultants, or by the graduate and undergraduate business schools.

Yet it is the public's ox that is being gored. And I believe it is the job of all of us in our own interests to see that—before we or any others add our bit to the fashionable scorn directed at this convenient scape-goat—we should be sure the facts and the record are checked to see if any proposed different arrangement can begin to measure up to what our private business system, with all its faults, is meanwhile yielding in current productivity and in potential for easing man's burdens.

Straightening ourselves out about profit in particular—and about private business in general—represents the greatest opportunity for quick advance in the level of living. This is by all odds the hardest job ahead for most of us—mentally, emotionally, and from the standpoint of proofing ourselves against the fallacious allurements of attractive untruths plied not only by the "Satans" quoting presumed or perverted Scripture for their purposes but also by the much too plentiful well-meaning but misled purveyors from stations both low and very high.

Probably the best opportunities for fruitful correction in this area can be found:

> in the presently unfiltered wishful thinking of the majority of us,
>
> in our store of damaging misinformation,
>
> in our deep-seated but unwarranted and very expensive prejudices acquired over our own lifetime on top of those handed down to us from prior generations,
>
> in our rationalization of immoral acts, and
>
> in our sophistication-deficiency which results in our allowing our representatives to operate on such a long leash that they are free to—and usually do—serve in greater or lesser degree their own personal economic or political interests to the harm of us constituents they are appearing to serve.

The specific corrections most of us need immediately to accomplish in our understanding of profit are such as these:

> Profit is not a cost to the consumer, but benefits the consumer through achieving prices which are much less than they would be if it were not for the profit-induced incentive to compete, to invest in improvements, and to manage efficiently,
>
> Profit does not cause inflation, but reduces the amount of inflation there would otherwise be,
>
> Profit is not "stolen", but is the earned reward

for efficiently supplying what customers want within a price at which less efficient competitors (the majority) are constantly going broke.

Profit is not the worker's enemy, but his best friend. For ⅛ of what is left after paying all outside expenses—the other ⅞ going to the worker—the investor supplies the arm-lengthening ideas and equipment which so largely take the work out of work, multiply the human output many times, and result in the ⅞ buying so much.

There is no job security like working for a low-cost producer and steady earner of profit adequate not only to promote sales at the currently competitive prices required but adequate also to warrant investment in growth and improvement which will enable the producer to keep up with—or ahead of—his domestic and foreign competition.

Profit is not "huge" or "exorbitant" or "swollen", but is surprisingly small not only compared with what others get from a business but also compared with the investor's contribution in doing typically 95% of the work for 5% of the sales dollar.

Profit is even smaller than reported in the annual statements of most companies, due to the improper treatment of depreciation and obsolescence required by the government in taxes and financial statements.

Profit does not go to just some few but goes *directly* to about 50,000,000 investors—involving half our families—and also *indirectly* to practically every man, woman and child in the U.S.

In short, profit is the driving force toward the greatly desired growth of jobs in numbers, in attractiveness, in promotional opportunities, in real pay, and in job security. Profit is the driving force likewise toward attractive value in wanted goods and services, and is the consumer's and even the poor man's best friend.

Yet profit desperately needs your help—in your own interests—whoever you are. There can no longer be any doubt that the new inflation of the late 60's, the freeze, and Phase II have all worked against profit being substantial enough either to supply adequate life blood to present investments or to create the ability and willingness to save and invest the further funds so needed now for the accomplishment of more attractive consumer values for the benefit of the whole public.

Profit has been going down for the past five years while inflationary pay went up spectacularly. Now *pay* can go on further up artificially by 5.5% a year, plus all sorts of adjustments for "catch-ups", "inequities" and other *politically* good reasons for exception. But *profit* is to get no 5.5 artificially raised ceiling and no "catch-ups", and even earned profit is to be held within the recently depressed rate.

The resulting damage to the public interest comes about simply because the public majority has let it become "good politics" for the majority's representatives in unions and in government to act that way. Phase II, *in concept*, is just as good as permitted by what was "good politics" at the moment and, *in administration*, it is going to prove just as good or bad as what is "good politics" with the majority will make it. And if it does not prove *pretty* good, the successor Phase III is going to be a whole lot rougher on citizens not only as investors but also as earners, consumers, home owners, and hopeful seekers after the better life generally.

If the politicians are reasonably correct about what the public wants or will permit—and they usually are—then it is pretty obvious that the public majority has not recently been, and is not now, equipped with the proper economic knowledge, moral fortification, and political sophistication to enable it to make decisions and take actions which really serve its own interests in the profit area.

Everyone of us citizens is highly obligated—in our very selfish interest as well as patriotically in our country's interest—to master the full range of the facts as to the good which investment and profit do for all, and then to help all within our possible reach to be similarly grounded beyond any chance of being fooled by Satans quoting perverted Scripture for their purposes.

It will not be possible for us to do this unless we really rid ourselves of the foolish idea so many of us have been successfully fed to the effect that private business is owned by just the few and that profit goes only to that few.

What is a Business?

A private business is not some one or few. It is itself *the many*. It has a unique purpose, nature and mechanics involving *always the many*.

A private business is a voluntary association of people in a sort of clearing house, where they come together to do *wanted* things for each other on a something-for-something basis. They voluntarily so associate because they can thus get more done for each other than if each were working alone with only the resources each could personally supply. They are enabled to do more for each other because of the investment, the superior ideas and the opportunity for specialization there.

A private business is not just buildings, or machinery, or inventory, or money. Business is primarily people . . . dealing with each other . . . with each willing to provide equal value in return for what he wants. Business thus concerns itself with *things* only through *people* . . . and then only as a result of people indicating they need or want those particular things.

One of the top marvels of all the world's history is the way we interdependent citizens have come together in business voluntarily, have so largely done for each other what each wants done in return for what he provides, and have in the process maintained our education and morals at a level that has permitted almost everybody to go around doing practically as he pleases without intruding unduly on the free choice and other rights, dignity, usefulness, economic progress and spiritual well-being of his fellow citizens.

The real mission of any private business—as well as the requirement for its survival to supply values and jobs—is to please people by helping them get all they have coming *on the basis of enlightened understanding* as to what they can reasonably expect from the business in both material and non-material ways. The key assignment by the public majority for itself is to be sure it has acquired that enlightened understanding and persists in seeing that things proceed in accordance with that understanding.*

Even bigness is not automatically bad. It fact, bigness and continued success *can* be and usually are *good* for the consumer, good for the employee, good for smaller businesses including their suppliers, distributors and even their smaller competitors. A big business obviously is good—though discomforting—for its big competitors by keeping them on their toes to improve competitive values.

---

* From the chapter on "The Mission of Business" in "THE TRUTH ABOUT BOULWARISM—Trying to do right voluntarily". (Bureau of National Affairs, Washington, D.C.)

In the process, let's look at what has happened in the area of the numbers of investors in private business. The profit-seeking investors in the United States now number about 50,000,000 citizens—involving half our families—who are *direct* owners of our 1,500,000 businesses. And the *indirect* investors in business are two to three times the *direct* owners (even after correcting for some duplication).

There are over 31,000,000 known owners of stock in *corporation's* listed on the exchanges. Half of them are women. There are millions more owners of stock in unlisted corporations, and there are over 10,000,000 *unincorporated* businesses having obviously many more than 10,000,000 owners. There are over 2,000,000 commercial farms which are, of course, profit seeking businesses owned by more than that number of people.

So there must be well over 50,000,000 citizens and their families who are *directly* interested in their business property being properly protected and its opportunity for usefulness being properly encouraged. Keep in mind that many companies have 25, 50 and even 75% of their employees as stockholders, so a very heavy percentage of our country's 80,000,000 civilian workers—along with their families—must be included in the 50,000,000 *direct* owners of business.

Then there are these further millions of savers who are *indirect* investors in business because their savings are being risked in business structures and obligations whose yield, worth and safety depend on the ability of business to offer attractive values while operating in an economic and political climate that helps business be useful to all: 28,200,000 participants in private pension funds, 130,000,000 insurance policy holders, depositors in 24,496,000 savings accounts, and other depositors in open bank accounts (no recent figures available, but they must now be over 50,0000,000).

Then—since the attacks on private business are essentially attacks on the freedom to own and use private property—there is the fact that more than half of our country's families own their own homes. These—and owners of the many other kinds of private property—have exactly the same inherent interest in the protection and productivity of their savings as do the direct and indirect investors in business.

Obviously, there are many duplications in the above figures because of a single saver and investor appearing more than once. But after all such duplications were identified, the result would still have to be that practically every man, woman and child has not one stake—but several stakes—in business being productive and healthy. Practically all citizens, once they know the facts, should in their own interests cooperate with business in two ways: (a) in *helping* business correct anything that *ought* to be corrected and (b) in helping business be then fully useful.

How Big are Profits

Then there is the perennial question of how big profits are—and if they are too big. This question has again been analyzed by the reliable Opinion Research Corporation, of Princeton, New Jersey, and reported thus in Business Week of December 18, 1971:

"AN INFLATED VIEW OF COMPANY PROFITS"

"In 1970, American manufacturing companies made a 4¢ after-tax profit on every dollar of sales. But according to a survey conducted by Mcgraw-Hill's Opinion Research Corp., the American people think manufacturing companies make 28¢ on every sales dollar after they pay taxes, seven times the actual figure. And it suggests that while corporations—and the press—have done a good job educating investors on stock values, they have done poorly in telling the public about the true state of profits.

"The professional researchers asked a statistically selected sample of 1,000 adults the following question: 'Just as a rough guess, what percent profit on each dollar of sales do you think the average manufacturer makes, after taxes?' Though the average of the responses was 28¢, the average woman guessed 34¢, and a special sample of teen-agers guessed 33¢. The purportedly astute stock owner guessed 23¢, better than the overall average but still about six times higher than the actual figure. Two categories, people with incomes over $15,000 a year and farmers, tied for the best average guess at 21¢.

"The ironic twist is that, even though the public's estimate of manufacturers' profitability is absurdly inflated, most think that current profits 'as a whole are reasonable.' Only 26% believe that business is making too much. On the other hand, Opinion Research notes that a growing number of Americans feel, *that company profits should be limited by government*. In this year's study, 33% of the adults felt this way, the highest figure the survey has recorded since 1948.

"Furthermore, the public holds a distorted view of the pressure of wage increases on profits. Two-thirds of the adults that were sampled believe that a 10¢ hourly wage increase can be paid by American companies without raising prices.

"EDUCATION NEEDED. The public's startling lack of knowledge concerning business profits is not unique to 1971, although the 28¢ figure is the highest Opinion Research has come up with in the 26 years it has taken the survey. In 1969's survey, the average public estimate was 27¢ per sales dollar compared

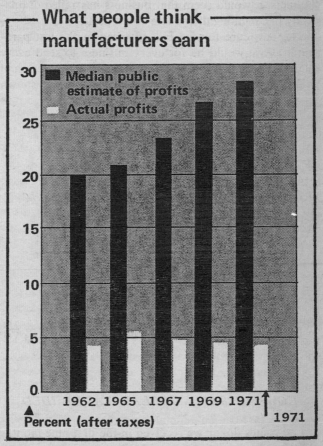

What people think manufacturers earn

Median public estimate of profits

Actual profits

1962 1965 1967 1969 1971

Percent (after taxes)

1971

Data: Opinion Research Corp., Federal Trade Commission, Securities & Exchange Commission with an actual profit slice of 4.8¢. The preceding year, the estimate was 23¢ compared with an actual of 5¢, and in its most accurate year, 1945, the public estimate was still some 3½ times higher than the actual profit margin.

"With public opinion bearing so little resemblance to the facts, it would seem that business has failed dramatically in educating the people about itself."

The best cure for the failure noted in the last paragraph above would be for every business to send every quarter to its employees, customers, stockholders and neighbors a statement along the lines of the one shown below and on the next page.

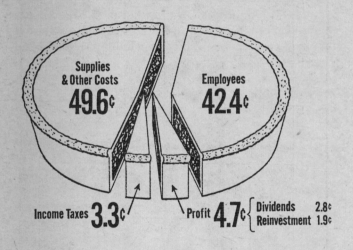

HOW THE SALES DOLLAR WAS DIVIDED

Each sales dollar we received in the first nine months of 1971 was divided as follows:

For Supplies—49.6 cents—the largest slice

For Income Taxes—3.3 cents

For Employees—42.4 cents—nine times profits.

For Profit—the 4.7 cents left—with 2.8 cents going to stockholders in dividends, and 1.9 cents held to cover inadequate depreciation and to meet investment needed for competitive strength and growth.

This may look like a lot of money, but it is only 4½% of sales and 11% as much as went for employees. Yet on it depends the sales and jobs of tomorrow.

In this connection, it is not just necessary for employees to know—but also for consumers, stockholders, editors, teachers, and other thought-leaders to keep clearly in mind—the ratio between pay and profit. Here is another kind of usable comparison for all business put out by the American Economic Foundation, 51 East 42nd Street, New York 10017:

Who Gets the Corporate Income?

Year	Employee Compensation	Pre-tax Profits	After-tax Profits
		Per cent of national income	
1965	69.8%	13.8%	8.2%
1966	70.2	13.6	8.0
1967	71.5	12.2	7.1
1968	72.4	12.3	6.7
1969	74.0	11.0	5.8
1970	75.6	9.5	5.2
1971 Jan.-June average	75.8	9.6	5.2

Source: July 1971 Survey of Current Business

A dramatic illustration of the need for corrected understanding by all concerned—and the vital obligation of businessmen to supply it in the interests of themselves and all their fellow citizens—is in the current attacks by politicians on the familiar old "profiteering midddlemen" resulting from the "discovery" that steak per pound at the butcher shop is some three times the price per pound of beef on the hoof at the farm. Conveniently omitted is any mention of the thousand and one services performed between farm and shop—with attendant high wages, waste and taxes and with resulting low or often no profit per service.

It happens that just as I was entering college in 1912 I was disillusioned at hearing a perennial Presidential candidate—whom I had previously admired from afar —tell farmers at a county fair that the difference in the prices of wheat and bread demonstrated how they were being robbed by the "interests". I am thus particularly indebted to the Tax Foundation for the following analysis of what happens to wheat from farm to bread—including the taxes injected at each stage—for I believe this will arm us to help our fellow citizens understand what happens to beef on the way to our broilers:

Taxes on a Loaf of Bread

The number of taxes that get into the cost of everything we buy was dramatically shown in a study made by the Tax Foundation, a private research organization. Their approach was a direct one: start counting the taxes. They started with a loaf of bread made and sold in Indianapolis. They limited the counting to the Federal and state taxes paid by the grocer, the baker, the companies making ingredients that went into the bread, and the railroads that hauled the ingredients.

The grocer paid four Federal taxes—individual income tax, tax on his telephone, tax on transportation of property and a tax on his safe deposit box. The baker, a national company owning its own trucks, paid eight Federal taxes—corporation income tax, stamp taxes on its security transfers, the telephone tax, the telegram tax, transportation tax for its salesmen, transportation tax for its product, the safe deposit tax and the social security tax.

The grocer and baker also paid 15 *state* taxes, with the bakery paying most of them because it was a corporation and because of the gasoline and motor vehicle taxes on its trucks. Included in the state taxes paid by the baker were four corporation taxes paid in Delaware where the company is chartered. Both grocer and baker paid an Indiana gross income tax.

That's not all. A Kansas City flour mill which supplied the baker paid seven Federal taxes and eight Missouri state taxes. And the railroad that brought the flour to Indianapolis paid five taxes to Uncle Sam and an assortment of taxes to Missouri, Illinois, and Indiana—the states crossed on this particular delivery.

Next, the sugar that went into the bread came from a large New Orleans refining company that paid eight Federal taxes and six Louisiana taxes. Then there were taxes paid by the railroad that hauled the sugar to Indianapolis, the salt warehouse in Chicago from which the salt came, the malt company in Chicago, the shortening manufacturer in Cincinnati, the milk solids company and the yeast factory, both in Chicago, and the railroads that carried these ingredients.

Assuming that all these outfits passed along part of their tax burden in prices, there were at least 151 taxes on this single loaf of bread sold by the Indianapolis grocer. No wonder the price of bread has doubled in 20 years or so.

The researchers of Tax Foundation followed this same "count 'em" procedure for other common items. They discovered there were at least:

100 taxes on an egg	150 taxes on a woman's hat
116 taxes on a man's suit	600 taxes on a house

This old deceitful charge has obviously continued to be "good politics" for the 60 years of my experience and probably longer. Yet the continued susceptibility of the public to such appeals means that the usefulness of business to all is being hampered. This and other false charges can be easily debunked if those who know the truth will give these misrepresentations the treatment they deserve in the public interest.

And it must be kept in mind that such false charges continue only because the enemies of our business system find it so easy to misrepresent costs and prices through conveniently disregarding the many expenses necessary between

1. The visible cost of some principal raw materials, and
2. The price of the finished product delivered to the consumer.

The uncorrected misrepresentation results in the public majority being vulnerable to charges that lots more useless expenses could be absorbed—or that a lot lower price is possible—all out of an unconscionable profit margin wrongly assumed.

Even the very best activities of business in the common interest are made to seem the worst—simply because business people and others have not been alerted to the need to correct such misrepresentation as a duty to themselves as workers, consumers and savers.

Just one of the prominent examples is safety. Obviously, performance by private parties will never be perfect—any more than government performance can be perfect—and anything still needing correction should be corrected with the promptness and to the degree possible in human affairs.

But what goes unnoticed is the way the enemies of our business and political system use safety charges to stir emotions while hiding the great good done in this area by business in contrast to the few continuing exceptions which are constantly being lessened.

While factories, for instance, are inherently more dangerous than most other places, the safety precautions taken by management—for both profit and humane reasons—have made the worker far safer there than on the way home, or at home, or on vacation. It has come almost to the point where the individual has to invent an unusual form of personal negligence in order to get hurt in most any typical modern place of business.

A further increase in safety is constantly being sought —again for both profit and humane reasons—but the remaining areas of possibly improved protection against personal negligence are near the vanishing point.

In all of industry in 1969 there were 14,000 accidental deaths. Of these only 1,900 occurred in the presumably more dangerous manufacturing area, and 80% of these resulted from human error and not from any lack of safety precautions supplied by business.

In the 1926-27 period the accident frequency was 35 per 1,000,000 man hours. By 1969 this was down to 8 per 1,000,000 man hours. And the severity had likewise gone way down.

Most of the states, particularly the industrial ones, have very stringent safety laws and, needless to say, the state officials recognize it as extremely "good politics" to enforce the regulations rigidly.

Yet—simply because the public majority hears only one side—it continues to be profitable politically to heap regulation upon regulation at the pointless expense of prices and jobs.

Just one latest evidence of this is the new *federal* Occupational Safety & Health Act (OSHA) of 1970. This is causing an enormous expenditure of money and effort needlessly heaped on top of the continuing state laws, bureaus and field inspectors. The presumed objective is to accomplish a result that is already being achieved by business and the states just as fast as humanly possible. Even then, the primary focus of this added new federal law is on administrative safety and health standards rather than on the elimination of human error which is the primary cause of those accidents which continue.

No one would want to stand in the way of any worthwhile improvement in safety however slight. But the sad fact in this situation is that the public is to pay an exhorbitant cost in prices and jobs with an infinitesimal, if any, improvement over what would take place anyhow.

In like vein, advertising continues a favorite whipping boy for the left-leaning politicians and others with anti-business interests. Here again the false charges are found useful simply because the public majority has not been supplied the facts about how advertising results in more jobs, lower prices, and higher satisfactions in both the material and non-material areas of living.

Because they have not been adequately informed to the contrary, too many people believe charges that advertising:

1. Is an "expensive parasite" which needlessly raises costs and prices in the interest only of unwarranted and anti-social profit,
2. Lessens competition and leads to monopoly,
3. Deceitfully or otherwise wrongly brainwashes helpless readers and listeners into buying products which they do not need or really want and which are not even as advertised.
4. Lowers taste and weakens morals of old and young by playing to the lowest common denominator in the public.

Nothing could be further from the facts.

To be sure, there are some misrepresentations, some bad taste and some other intended or unintended wrong-doing in some advertising—just as such is to be found in the course of human affairs elsewhere.

But these are exceptions to the general rule, and do not last long. The untruthful advertising soon disappears with the untruthful advertiser. This is by action of buyers who find they have been misled. Certainly this retribution is sometimes a little later than it should be even by a more or less careless consuming public, and there is both an opportunity and an obligation for the buyer to shorten the elapsed time in his own interest.

But meanwhile the great bulk of advertising is doing an extremely valuable job for workers, consumers and savers alike. For

1. Advertising supplies the buyer with valuable time-saving and travel-saving information as to what is available, what it does, what its price is, and where it can be bought. (Even a presidential candidate was jokingly reported to have finally gone to "The Yellow Pages" to find a running mate.)

2. Advertising cuts sharply the distribution expense of time and travel for wholesale and retail salesmen.

3. Advertising makes possible the wide enough sale to enable the producer to cut the cost of production while providing steady jobs.

4. The surviving advertiser gives the buyer a valuable assurance of quality and service.

5. Advertising pays almost entirely the bill for the news, sports, and entertainment which the public enjoys at minimum expense in newspapers and at no expense on TV and radio.

6. In addition to the above savings—which flow through to the consumer in prices and other expenses much lower than they otherwise could be—advertising performs an additional service in the area of the extra human satisfactions which the socialists criticize but which the public loves—*in fact, very largely lives for.*

In our affluent society, most people have been judged to be working about one hour a day to supply the *basic material* satisfactions from food for sustenance, clothing for covering, and housing for shelter; they are thought to work the other seven hours for the *extra human* satisfactions in the non-material fields derived not only from the product itself—in its form, color, taste, aroma, convenience, distinction, and other emotional or esthetic attributes—but also from the supplier's manners in dealing and associating with the buyer.*

---

* See Chapter 3 of THE TRUTH ABOUT BOULWARISM.

Advertising is a very important force in teaching where to secure and how to enjoy these extra human satisfactions sought.

The whole story of advertising's usefullness to workers, consumers and savers can not begin to be covered in the space available here. But complete and excellent information is available from both the American Association of Advertising Agencies, 200 Park Avenue, New York, N.Y. 10017 and from the Association of National Advertisers, 155 East 44th Street, New York, N.Y. 10017.*

Individual businesses—whether or not substantial advertisers themselves—have a vital stake in turning back this attack which is being made on our system through the effort to discredit advertising. They need—in their own and the common interest—to disseminate the corrective information through their employees, customers, stockholders and community neighbors.

And the individual citizen has the obligation—in his own interests—to correct his own ideas and help all his associates, friends and neighbors correct theirs.

---

* Also see Professor Israel M. Kirzner's article on ADVERTISING in the FREEMAN MAGAZINE, September, 1972.

Time to Act

The Freeman Magazine quotes John Chamberlain in his "Roots of Capitalism" as saying:

"Profits . . . are the special creation of the ability, the know-how, the inventiveness, the foresight, the imagination, of the superior executive. They are, in effect, not added to the price but *taken out of cost.*"

But the intentional and unintentional enemies of private business are yet able to play for keeps with a public majority which unfortunately still lacks the facts as to the good which business does as well as how it does that good.

We all need to hurry to change that. For private property and personal freedom are possible only where there are the incentives and rewards—perils and security—of a profit-and-loss economy disciplined by an informed and alerted public majority.

Chapter V

THE COLLECTIVE BARGAINING REQUIREMENT

I may seem late in getting to the subject on which my original invitation was based. But I have wanted to make it clear ahead of time how I believe the public's bargaining problem points to and fits into the public's larger overall problem not only of solving the immediate inflation, unemployment, productivity and profit difficulties but also of preserving freedom and moving on up to the better life in the process.

So I have discussed the "prior homework" which the public should require its representatives in business management to do not only for equity in periodic bargaining but, more importantly, for optimum productivity all along. I have suggested the economic understanding, moral fortification and political sophistication which the individual citizen needs in order to be able to think and act competently about such matters affecting his interests and obligations as worker, consumer and saver.

We now come to the next requirement as to what the individual citizen needs to learn and do—and needs so largely to be *helped* to learn and do—about the particular effect which present day bargaining is having on his worker, consumer and saver interests.

I am assuming that every serious student of the current collective bargaining scene is searching for the answer not only to why this theoretically good process has gone so far astray in practice, but also to who can and should do what about it.

My purpose here is hopefully to contribute something worthwhile for the good of the cause by bringing out into the open some assumptions and practices previously considered so sacrosanct as to permit of no re-examination. For the situation has now advanced to the point where it seems the affected citizens must be willing to take a needed look at their own responsibility for so much of what they quite properly do not like.

Business was once free of restraint, got too powerful, abused that power, and had to be brought under control by the public. The question needing examination now is whether or not labor union power has reached that same stage.

My views on this subject are still unfashionably apart from the current consensus, although probably not nearly as far apart as they would have been from the consensus of a little earlier. In any event, I feel sure I was invited precisely because my kind of observations are still so hard to come by in public that most discussions of this subject are limited to just the one side and do not include the other to make them the balanced dialogues they should be.

Let's look at what has been going on. Back in 1935 the public majority intended to establish and support a balance of strength as between employees and their employers, and to encourage settling pay and working-condition differences through good faith bargaining between two parties who would each be equally free to accept or reject the proposals of the other.

The public's objective was for the individual employee to have available every means that might be needed to enable him to get surely all of—but certainly not more than—what was equitably coming to him in return for his contribution. His take was thus to be unfailingly up even with what others were getting in return for their contributions to him.

Labor unions were to be freely available where a majority of employees so desired, and it must have been expected that union members and their representatives would, to their own evident advantage, cooperate with management and the public authorities in arriving at arrangements which were genuinely equitable and destined to aid the employer, rather than interfere with him,

in making jobs attractive, numerous and stable within the market price he could collect from customers,

in his doing so while at the same time serving, and not detracting from, the *balanced* best interests of all citizens in their concurrent roles as earners, consumers, savers and freemen.

Such an underlying concept of unions was and is certainly good.

In the early stages, the unions served well in the human considerations area by pointedly alerting managers to the need and desirability of abandoning any sins of neglect on the one hand and of any paternalism on the other, and of developing instead a genuine two-way human relationship which would prove mutually rewarding.

Likewise, in the economic area, the unions did good early work in persuading or forcing any backward employers to bring their employees up even with going market pay.

But after that promising beginning in both the human relations and economic considerations areas, the union officials quickly began going far afield in the use of the force which the public had put in their hands. Through the huge funds automatically available—and through unrealistic promises of something-for-nothing which they claimed they could win for members, and even for the public majority, through forcible extraction from an unworthy minority—they built up an overwhelming political power which the public did and does not intend but which the public majority as yet too little recognizes is what has really come about.

Two results of this growth of political power need broad understanding. The first is that the union officials have gained political and economic dominance over employers, public, governments and even employees. The second is that they have become a principal engine of inflation through forcing pay far above productivity and then forcing government to inflate in order to delay as much as possible the inevitable job-killing effects of this thoroughly impractical procedure.

Thus the union program has shifted from an intimate economic and human dignity bargaining table matter on its merits to predominantly a far-flung political process. This means that both management and union representatives—and government or other third parties—have to be guided by what the public majority rightly or wrongly orders or permits.

The union officials have recognized all this quite fully. Before arrival at the bargaining table they have usually so done directly and through allies the required "prior homework" with employees and other public that they are characteristically in complete charge of the negotiations.

In contrast, management has too usually been not even alert to the political as well as other need for being sure it had first deserved—and then proceeded rightfully to achieve—that credibility with employees and other public which is a necessary aid to their calm examination of the issues and claims, their determining where equity really resides, and their contributing toward a workable settlement in the balanced best interests of all concerned. Even in the face of the constant and obviously damaging charge about their being one or another kind of brute, crook and exploiter of the deserving many for the benefit of some undeserving few, the owners and managers have been so silent as to leave their personnel and other public with the impression they were confessing guilt as charged.

As a result, our country's so-called "free collective bargaining" turns out today to be not free, not collective and, in fact, too one-sided to be any real bargaining at all.

What too usually goes for bargaining today is simply the imposition of a settlement which—no matter how camouflaged—is, in the end, substantially what the union official has unilaterally decreed or decided, with the employer simply "surrendering on each bargaining issue with supreme dignity."

Usually an unsound settlement imposed *directly* by a union official is substantially the same as it would have been if accomplished *indirectly* through a mediator, arbitrator, professional "fixer" type of go-between, committee of so-called "public" representatives, or White House agent under either the Democrats or Republicans.

The public majority cannot blame either the union officials or the third parties for what they do in such cases. Any unsound settlement they engineer will almost certainly be found in keeping with *effective* public opinion—that is, it has public approval, or it will be tolerated by the public, or will go unknown to the public, and the politicians involved are confident it will not stir up the active disfavor of the political majority if it does become known. In other words, such an unsound settlement comes within what is "good politics" with the public majority even though bad for that majority.

And we have to face the fact that any substantially different settlement in the circumstances would likely backfire on the union officials involved. That is because it would not stick with the employees and neighbors due either to what they already believe or to what they would quickly be taught to believe by the omnipresent political competitors of the particular union officials involved. Of course, this would not apply if a different and sounder settlement had meanwhile been made "good politics", but that is an unlikely development in the usual emotional atmosphere and in the very short time available for such corrective teaching during the formal bargaining period.

I am confident that many, many union officials now privately wish that less inflationary, less debilitating and more sensible settlements were possible—this in the interests not only of the members in particular but of the country in general. But these union officials—as politicians—have to go along with the whirlwind which they had a part in generating but never expected to reach its present proportions.

I am likewise confident that the majority of legislators, administrators, policemen and police chiefs, judges and juries would like to be able to abandon the now politically necessary double standard and, instead, have the law apply to all alike. But they dare not move in that direction—or even admit their wish to do so—until such a step has become "good politics."

Thus again, the needed correction is squarely up to the public majority on its own—with only such help as it can get largely from heretofore unaccustomed sources.

LUDWIG von MISES—that greatest living, if not all-time, economist—gives this wise counsel:

"A government that sets out to abolish market prices is inevitably driven towards the abolition of private property; it has to recognize there is no middle way between the system of private property in the means of production combined with free contract, and the system of common ownership of the means of production. . . . It is gradually forced towards compulsory production, universal obligation to labor, rationing of consumption and finally, official regulation of the whole of production and consumption."

The first thing I believe each member of the currently ruling majority needs to do in his own interest is to look in the mirror and ask the fellow he sees there if he is or is not acting wisely and responsibly in accordance with the tenents of his freedom and well being when he continues to be a party to giving the union officials their present imbalance of power through his being a party to the following:

1. Monopoly

The public majority—through its government's bad laws and worse administration of those bad laws—continues to give unions the opportunity to have a monopoly of an employer's labor market, while not effectively regulating that monopoly as to prices and practices in the way every other such legalized monopoly is regulated.

Union officials themselves are extremely vocal in attacking the evils of monopoly in the hands of others. But an unregulated monopoly here has to be just as bad as an unregulated monopoly anywhere else. The work done by people cannot be taken out of competition. A monopoly of 50% or 75% of the cost ingredients of a product or service is the same in principle—and relatively just as expensive—as a monopoly of the whole product or service. And in practice, the result has proved to be high costs, unattractive prices, unemployment, and stunted or negative growth in the number and attractiveness of future jobs.

As Dr. von Mises warns—and as the trend leading up to the present crisis confirms—the public majority has only two opposite choices and no middle ground. Either bargaining must be brought up to where a viable free-market price of labor is arranged between buyers and sellers having substantially equal rights, or government must fix the price of every job.

And government openly taking over such a dictatorial job would in itself provide no answer to the problems. For the politicians acting alone would have to continue responsive to the public majority's misconceptions and would thus necessarily continue with just as bad a job as the union politicians and government politicians combined have been doing to bring us to this crisis.

The only answer is for the public majority to escape from its old habit of mind and action and both wake up to why pricing in this field *should* be done—and then see that it *is* done—in the same way that has brought us our consumer progress in the product pricing field. Only the public majority can do this.

2. Compulsion

The public majority—again through its government's laws and their administration—continues to promote compulsory union membership in the name of "union security".

The security turns out almost always to be not for the union members against their employer but for the union official against his members. It insures an entrenched position for the union official, and leaves the members with little chance of redress for abuses or laxity by the official. As Supreme Court Justice Louis D. Brandeis put it:

> "A nucleus of unorganized labor will check oppression by the union as the union checks oppression by the employer".

The whole basis of our freedom is that the public majority will itself protect the minority against any unrestricted majority rule, and especially against any tyranny of the majority.

The very presence of a compulsory membership requirement makes it almost impossible to have a good union genuinely responsive to its members even in the unlikely event there should be 100% voluntary membership.*

Compulsory membership not only gives union officials the vast flow of funds to use legally and illegally for political activities in building and maintaining power which changes the nature of our government and free society. It also gives union officials the freedom to use the funds as they choose without member direction and

* See pages 127 to 133 of "The Truth About Boulwarism".

even contrary to the expressed wishes of large numbers of those forced to supply the funds.

Compulsory membership even provides the *employer* with the privilege of temporarily escaping the cost to him of some threatened damage and harassment if he will agree with the union officials to require an otherwise unwilling employee to pay money and subservience to that union as the price of holding his job with that employer.

This compulsory unionism is at both the immediate and long term expense of employees and other public, as well as at the long-term expense of the employer.

In addition, the public majority thereby gives union officials the free flow of millions which are used largely to dominate public opinion formation and thereby dominate government, business and the union members themselves along with the rest of the public.

This awesome political machine is reported to be using—both legally and with openly privileged illegality—enormous sums and the attendant vast field organization in such significant ways as these: (a) to usurp most of the media and other educational channels to the point of being practically the determining influence on public opinion in general and even about such matters now as inflation, unemployment, productivity and profit, (b) to lobby daily with already obligated or frightened Congressmen, Senators and other national, state and local public servants, and (c) to invest all year round in grass roots political spade work to destroy enemies and elect and re-elect willing allies to public office.

This is not only increasing greatly the cost of anyone in either party running for office. It is also, and much more importantly, warping the flow of public information and thus the impressions on which the public bases its decisions and actions in economic and moral matters as well as in the political field.

Repeated surveys show that a two-to-one public majority opposes the employer forcing the employee to pay tribute to a union as the price of holding a job with that employer. Yet the public does not fully appreciate the consequences to itself and thus does not properly rise to instruct its representatives. Accordingly, the latter are left free to respond to what is "good politics" with the union officials and their allies.

It would seem obvious that the public majority needs to do three things: First, stop the forced membership and its attendant subservience. Second, stem the flow of forced contributions to purposes so largely undesirable. Third, see that a better balance of economic, moral and political information is restored to all concerned as the basis for important day-to-day decisions and actions.

3. Privileged Violence

The public majority—through the active or passive force of its majority public opinion on administrators, courts and public media—succeeds in imposing the "good politics" requirement that its national, state and local law-enforcement agents allow union-connected threats and acts of violence to persons and property to go unimpeded and unpunished. This is a law-breaking privilege granted no other persons or institutions with public approval.

Union-connected violence may outwardly appear to be lessening. But, in fact, it is increasingly effective. The reason is that the appreciation of uninhibited union ability and willingness to commit violent acts with impunity is so widespread—and redress known to be so lacking—that most owners, managers, consumers and workers respond to the actual or implied threat of violence and do as they are told. This wide open opportunity—and proved willingness—to use the privileged violence has brought a result the public majority surely did not intend, does not yet sense, and would not permit if understood. For, as the distinguished observer, Arthur Krock stated last August:

"The picket line is now the supreme law of the land".

Let me emphasize again that I do not believe we can blame the politicians in unions for taking advantage of these political opportunities served up to them by a public majority which is overly well-meaning but also overly unobservant or neglectful or unsophisticated for its own good.

And the political process being what it is, we should not be surprised or resentful that the public majority's government representatives see it as "good politics" to give the union officials what they want and not to interfere with what the public majority actively or passively seems to regard, no matter how wrongly, as an excusable means to a presumed good end.

The affected individuals making up the public majority need, in their own interests, to advise their representatives in unions and in government that it is no longer "good politics"—and no longer even tolerable—for union officials or agents or allies to engage in illegal threats or acts of violence to persons and property.

4. The Myth of Union Weakness

Long after just the opposite should have become obvious to all, the public majority strangely persists in assuming union bargainers to be pitifully weak in the face of the employer's supposedly insuperable strength. Heightened by union persuasion amid management silence, this even extends to the impression that getting and keeping the employee up even with his employer at the bargaining table not only has not yet been accomplished but also continues so huge, so difficult and so urgent an undertaking that the costly consequences of *any* means, which even *appear* to serve that end, are to be suffered and excused.

There are only two things wrong with this. One is that the means being employed do not lead to the end promised. The other is, of course, that union power has long since gone far beyond any employer power and has mounted to where it dominates not only the employer but also government, education, press and air communications—and even to the point where the union official has too usually become the actual master of his members instead of their intended and presumed servant.

5. More Pay For No More Output

The public majority continues to honor the myth that arbitrary pay increases—without added output to match—can be met out of profits or out of capital.

This is the ultimate in cruel and nervy deception. Its chance of being believed depends entirely on lack of continuous access to the facts by the employee and other public majority—as has been covered here earlier.

The thus misled public majority continues to be slanted in favor of those things which union agents do and successfully persuade others to do, but which go unrecognized by the public majority as having results contrary to those promised workers, consumers and savers.

The union apparatus—with all too much help from business silence—has managed to keep the employee and public majority misinformed especially as to the high-wage and low-productivity influence on inflation and unemployment and as to the small size of profits in relation both to pay and to the good which profit does in providing better values for union members as well as for the rest of the public including the poor.

In a free society—or under a dictator—consumers have to pay the cost of production in the end. The public majority needs to correct its information and increase its sophistication to the point of warning its representatives in unions, government and business that it is wise to the absurdity of claims that unearned wage increases can be paid out of anything but higher consumer prices.

As just one example of what the negligent public tolerance is doing to the public interest, it has just been reported that union power decrees 42 men at an east coast port here to do what 5 men do on the other side of the Atlantic at Rotterdam.

After all, workers are not dealing with their employer. They are *dealing with themselves—through* their employer. What inescapably has to be done is to stop *forcing* pay above the market price which sovereign buyers and sellers would willingly determine on the basis of *worth* in free exchange.

Pay artifically forced above the market—and with no matching addition to output—is not only inflationary but is debilitating to the worker himself not only as a worker but also as the consumer and saver he is. Likewise, so-called "cost-of-living" increases in pay are just as inflationary and debilitating.

To bring this senseless procedure to an end will require both kinds of increases to be slowed down until productivity catches up. Even then the workers will be still better off if most of the economy's productivity increase is diffused to the public in prices rather than trying to accomplish this through wages.

Meanwhile, the union's proper role—in the interest of members as well as the rest of the public—is to see that the members do get the going market price and not that a new higher price is forcibly set to the damage alike of union members and the rest of the public.

6. Brutes, Crooks, Exploiters

The public majority—despite ample evidence to the contrary—keeps giving credence to the false claims that owners and managers are brutes, crooks and exploiters, and that cooperating with them is against employee and other public interest.

The owners and other financial backers of business are not some few rich. As earlier indicated, they are practically everybody. They are not different, but the same sort of folks as oneself—the folks one sees at church, school meetings, bars, bowling alleys, ball games, the next desk or work bench, *and when looking in the mirror.*

These people—including the worker participants—are the real benefactors of the worker. They take 95% of the work out of work and make possible our high level of living.

The managers—and the rest of the top 10% who supply and transmit the ideas which make jobs survive—are the same kind of well-intentioned folks.

There are undoubtedly the usual run of exceptions inescapable in human affairs, but they *are exceptions* to the overwhelming rule of constructive and conscientious conduct by most businessmen.

The very last thing the employee should do is to let his representatives or his own unwarranted prejudices persuade him to hate his work and to go around mad and miserable when he should recognize that he is enjoying the best lot which has ever been devised and which he himself can help improve.

As already indicated, the public majority should see to it that owners and managers are doing their level best —within their human-being limitations—to fix anything that should and can be fixed.

Then all-concerned, in even their own very selfish interests, should cooperate not only by helping to do that fixing but also by joining in to give every possible aid to accomplishing the attractive values in cost and quality which mean sales, jobs and a higher level of living.

Despite its human shortcomings, the private business system is still the greatest producer of human betterment ever yet conceived, and no one in his right mind should be guilty of anything like "throwing the baby out with the bath water".

7. Subsidizing Strikers Against the Public

The public majority is permitting—at its own expense—its governments and other agencies to refund to striking public and other employees most of the strikers' immediate personal cost.

The public is thus unwittingly financing strikes against itself—through such unsound practices as the misuse of food stamps, allowing unintended "welfare" payments, paying strikers as though "unemployed", having banks, merchants and others give unusual credit to the strikers, taking up local and national collections from other union members, school children, and church groups, and securing loans and gifts (they are frequently the same) from either national and local union treasuries.

Emphasizing the extent and cost of such unwise political favors, is the reproduction permitted here—from the timely and revealing new book Welfare and Strikes*

---

* University of Pennsylvania Press.

9. Coalition Bargaining

The public majority continues to supply government sanction and public opinion support for

Permitting the bargaining agent to be one or a few or several crafts in a company, a community or an entire industry—whichever best suits the strategies of the union officials involved—despite this choice too usually giving the union side the opportuntiy to precipitate an unwarranted crisis country-wide.

Bargaining by a coalition of unions in a company, or community or entire industry—at the pleasure of the unions—which last again can usually produce a country-wide crisis and also greatly affect a given company's or industry's ability to compete and supply jobs.

Bargaining by a closely-knit group of craft or other unions dealing with a large number of small competitors where the imbalance of power is so great as to make any idea of collective bargaining a travesty.

The above privileges and others like them have been secured from government by the unions in order that they may choose the arrangement or grouping which will give them the greatest and easiest excess of power to use in forcing the particular employers into a settlement politically satisfying for the union officials while too generally being economically destructive of consumer and investor interest at once and of employee interest at once or soon.

The hard fact is that in most such cases the excess of union power will prove to be basically just about the same no matter what grouping is used, and that it is merely easier for the union officials to apply that power as the group involved is larger.

The remedy for this situation is thus not in government arbitrarily imposing some particular grouping of the bargaining unit or in otherwise denying freedom of the parties to choose the grouping provided that freedom is surely shared equally by the parties. The remedy can only come from the public majority gaining the knowledge and alertness necessary to discipline the negotiators—*wherever* they are bargaining—to stay away from extraneous union political considerations and arrive at a settlement that is in the balanced best interests of all concerned.

This is not, however, to deny the fact that—from the standpoint of the members—the distribution of the employment cost available can usually be done more to the individual employee's own interest and liking as the bargaining units become smaller and confined to a part or all of a single employer's local work force.

10. Two Interest Gaps

The public majority is a party—directly and through government—to failure to recognize and deal properly in the public interest with two widening gaps between the interests of employees and those of union officials.

The first of these is the wide and still widening gap between the *economic* interests of union members and the *political* interests of the union officials.

The second is the wide and rapidly widening gap between the union officials objectives for all "labor," and the non-union workers' ideas as to what would help them maximize their opportunity for individual usefulness and consequent earned reward.

The persistence of the U.S. Labor Department over

the years in catering practically exclusively to the demands and wishes of union officials—and in doing so openly to try to get the top union officialdom's election help or other political support for the Democratic or Republican administration in power—is a sad commentary on the morals required of our politicians and on the public majority's lack of political sophistication.

If it were the 19 million unionized workers who were temporarily getting the benefit—at the expense of the 68 million workers who have succeeded in staying out of unions—that would be *pretty* bad. But to have most all this activity not really be aimed at economically benefitting even the unionized workers—but at politically pleasing the relatively few union officials—has always seemed to me to be *awfully* bad.

· For twenty-four years I have been publicly and privately contending that there should be two labor departments. The present one would be called the "Union Labor Department". The other—three times as big— would be called the "Non-Union Labor Department."

Since only a fourth of the work force is now in unions —and since only numbers count in politics—I believe the politician who has the courage to propose this will start with a 3 to 1 advantage. The public majority should start promising such advantage. But how deeply ingrained is this habit of government to favor union officials because of political hopes or fears—and how dulled the electorate still is to this unfair and injurious practice—has just been demonstrated again in the appointment of only union officials to the labor side of the Pay Board despite their representing only a fourth of the work force.

To be sure this—plus the early rulings—produced an unprecedented outcry that the Pay Board was favoring the union position and operating as a union organizing

agency. But when the four union officials walked off—
and it was suggested that some representatives of the
75% unorganized be appointed in their stead—it was
obvious that any such appointment is still rated as politically impractical.

The public majority, in its own interest, would seem
more than warranted in having government prove it is
openly and genuinely pursuing the interests of all workers alike.

The National Labor Relations Board has been similarly guilty. But this seems to have at last been recognized and some slight improvement begun. Let us hope
that this is the beginning of the really big correction
needed. The public majority cannot serve its interests
any better than by seeing that this *is* done.

Likewise, after almost forty years of generally favoring the union position right or wrong, the Supreme
Court has recently shown some indication of moving up
again toward a proper balance in union-management
cases. Let us hope that here, too, the needed correction
continues.

Our government has long had another politically convenient bad habit. It has opened the way for misrepresentation in favor of unwarranted claims from union
sources. And this habit of government is now adversely
affecting the stabilization efforts which the government
itself is making in the public interest. It is the habit of
publicly releasing the increases in the price index without likewise—at the same time and *in the same release*
—reporting the obviously related rise in wages.

As a consequence, most everyone is left with the er-
roneous impression that prices have been, and are, rising faster than incomes. One expert now points out in
April, 1972 the contrasting fact that ever since July
1971—the month before the freeze—average non-farm
wages have increased twice as fast as the price index,

retail wages three times as fast, and construction wages (even from their high base) about three times as fast.

This is still far from good enough. But at this early stage in the effort to wind down our wage and price inflation, this may represent not too bad progress toward the Administration's interim target of 5.5% wage increases with a 2 to 3% price rise. The point here at the moment, however, is that the facts are exactly the opposite of the charges, that progress is being made, and that we must meanwhile avoid letting irresponsible claims about prices rising faster than wages mislead us into decisions and actions contrary to our interest.

It is to be hoped (April 1972) that government will soon be convinced from the grass roots that it is no longer "good politics" to shelter such actual or potential misrepresentation by silence or omission. The public majority should give its representatives the proper instructions and support for the helpful change from the current practice.

11. Government's Own Sedition

The public majority—directly and through its government—is promoting the unionization of police, garbagemen, teachers, firemen and the rest of the 16 million government employees on a basis which is dangerous to persons, homes, other property and government itself, as well as warping the country's educational, moral and political processes.

Politicians—with no protest from the public majority —have generally judged it "good politics" to aid organizers in unionizing ever more of this vast army of federal, state and local government employees—and in doing so on the same basis as the business employees are organized.

Certainly no one should think of denying government employees the same access which other employees have to collective bargaining where such employees decide they need or want it as a means of insuring genuine equity for themselves.

But what the public majority is promoting or permitting is bringing even to government employees the same union teaching and practices which have become so damagingly prevalent with the unionization of business employees and which become all the more damaging in the area of government employment.

Policemen, firemen, garbage collectors and transportation workers are now being taught they should—and shown they can with impunity—engage in the precise destruction of life, health and property which they are hired to protect.

This takes it from what was formerly just "good politics"—to now being in keeping with their own personal creed—for them to stand idly by when others are threatening or damaging the freedom, lives, homes and other savings of their fellow citizens and—without their seeming to realize it—*of themselves*. The situation now and for the recent past in New York, for instance, is eloquent of how those charged with teaching and enforcing law have no intention of respecting or obeying the law themselves.

A historic case—and a vivid illustration of how teachers are being led to adopt and support force as a substitute for voluntarism in getting what you think you have coming—is that of Mrs. Carol Applegate who was fired from a Michigan school system because she could not in conscience pay compulsory fees. She sued and got a recent ruling that she was unlawfully fired, but that decision is expected to be appealed. She says in part:

"Is academic freedom a fragile hope, easily crushed by the teacher union professionals among us?"

"As one who has worked with the minds of the young for over 20 years, I have witnessed the insidious plague of compulsory unionism spread among the teachers of Michigan.

With it comes direct threat to our academic freedom and the pressure to politicize our academic and university system.

The only way we can be sure of a free America is by having students who are taught to think by teachers who are allowed to think."

Teachers in schools, colleges and universities are being taught—and are teaching their students—the something-for-*nothing* brand of economics, morals and politics which calls for trying to get what you want in the destructive way through threats of gang force or through acts of violence.

Our freedom was founded—and both our material and non-material welfare has been built—on the *constructive* something-for-*something* brand of realistic economics, honest morals, and sophisticated politics which—both in the practice and in the breach—has proved for two centuries that the only way really to get what you want is not by force but by *worth* as determined in voluntary exchange among willing buyers and sellers.

Yet this vast army, which *is* government, is being persuaded to be *against* government—that is, against *itself*—as a brute, crook and exploiter. In the process—as in unionized business employment—this vast army is being taught to be against our whole system of free choice, personal savings, individual responsibility, limited government, incentives to excellence, and rewards *from* others being based on worth *to* others.

The remedy is not to deny collective bargaining to public servants who want it. Nor will abridgment of the right to strike—combined with the substitution of compulsory arbitration—provide *in itself* the answer. For the arbitration findings will have to be political rather than economic—and thus will continue the currently damaging process—as long as the *basic* trouble persists.

The cure can come only from remedying that basic defect which now prevents collective bargaining from properly serving government employees, business employees and the rest of the public. That remedy is in corrective economic, moral and political education being *extensive* enough—and of the resulting pressure of sophisticated majority opinion being *intensive* enough—to bring the parties to the bargaining table with as little real and supportable difference in judgment as to the proper price as is customary between commercial buyers and sellers.

Then, if arbitration as a substitute for the strike should still be considered necessary or desirable, such arbitration could and would be done fairly and soundly in keeping with the going market price applicable. Any attempted distortion of the market would ignite backfire from a public majority which recognizes the error and knows that workers, consumers and savers would be paying the economic and social cost of an unwarranted settlement whether too high or too low.

Meanwhile, the public majority needs to see that its army of public servants is not taught to hate and permitted to impede or tear down the system they are hired to protect and run. Trying to "divide the wealth" on an arbitrary something-for-nothing basis simply results in the wealth disappearing. The way, in contrast, to maximize the benefits of wealth is to put it to work. The way for public servants to do their part in this is to encourage and protect savers in both the creation of savings and in the risking of those savings in the arm-lengthening processes now so needed.

Here, as in business, the employees in their own interests should not "throw the baby out with the bath water" but should *help* fix the exceptions and meanwhile *cooperate* in making our still best of all systems work.

12. *Other Abuses Publicly Sanctioned*

The public majority needs now almost a year later to ponder seriously the following two paragraphs from a Wall Street Journal editorial of July 26, 1971:

"In the past four decades, especially, unions have enjoyed strong political support. Government has helped them to organize major industries and t keep the industries organized. Friendly laws an, more important, friendly administration of those laws have helped to build union power. For a long time the so-called union movement was a favorite liberal cause, since it supposedly advanced the interests of the working man. Only recently have some of the politicians begun to realize exactly what it is that they have helped to create.

Whatever the aims of early leaders, organized labor now is primarily concerned with preserving and increasing its own power. There's nothing remarkable about this; as social institutions mature their own needs always begin to override their original purposes."

In this connection, the following further past and

current practices of its government would seem each to require the public majority's specific review as to whether or not contributing to the public's own mounting revolt now over unexpectedly poor values and prospects:

The old Railway Labor Acts calls for a ritual which is largely for public consumption. It routes a dispute past intermediate points of presumed bargaining. But no real bargaining can be expected to take place along the way, since the seasoned participants know the dispute will inevitably land in the lap of a board appointed by the White House. In view of the political pressures involved in the appointment and operation of such a panel, its recommendations can hardly be expected to turn out other than the heavily-compromised, uneconomic, and union-favoring ones they so generally prove to be. As a result of the public majority permitting such, its consumer values, worker jobs and quality of life are the poorer.

The old Wagner Act—despite its Taft-Hartley amendments—continues to be interpreted as a public command for government to put its power not only behind the organization of willing joiners but also into helping the organizers force workers into unions even against their will while employers are kept practically silent and the police are made to tolerate violence to the public's persons and property as "good politics" with the public. For a long time, the National Labor Relations Board conveniently ignored the Taft-Hartley correction which decreed that the right to refrain from joining a union is equal to the right to join. As already indicated, the NLRB has recently shown some hopeful signs of changing to fairness in the interpretation of this law. But there is still a long way to go. And as a result of the public permitting the continuance of abuses meanwhile, its prices, jobs and quality of life are the poorer.

Other labor laws contributing to excess union power—such as local and state laws, plus Bacon-Davis, Walsh-Healey, and McNamara-O'Hara—raise costs artificially, have a broad pattern-setting effect, and should be repealed in worker and other public interest. Because of the public majority permitting them to continue, its consumer values, worker jobs and quality of life are the poorer.

Broad exemptions for unions are still enjoyed under the anti-trust laws and the Norris-Laguardia Act. Until lately the unions were even protected by Norris-Laguardia from injunctions in union breach of contract actions. This legal immunization by the public has resulted in poorer values, jobs and quality of life.

The Full Employment Act of 1946 not only fails miserably its intended purpose but also is a basic instigator of our chronic and debilitating inflation. Meanwhile it increases the imbalance of union power by fostering further harmful monopoly. This law thus further impairs values, jobs and the quality of life.

Boards such as the National War Labor and the Wage Stabilization ones had to operate in World War II in accordance with unfortunate political necessities in the face of the union demands, instead of having the understanding support of the public in doing what was in the balanced best interests of all in that public. As a result of the affected public then permitting such, we have today a greater accumulation of inflation—and a continuing damage to values, jobs and freedom—from the pattern set back there by the war-time pay being so much beyond any production of producer and consumer goods to match.

The recent Pay Board—while the first genuinely tri-partite one—still had to keep its corrective decisions within what would have majority public understanding, approval and support, else those decisions would backfire and be upset. Unfortunately the public majority understanding was not yet up to what would be for the public's own good, and thus many of the decisions—while in the right direction—had to stop short of what would have been fully corrective in the public interest.

The improper freedom from competition allowed labor unions under the unwise laws and the indulgent NLRB interpretations—in contrast to the quite proper insistence on employer competition under the rigidly enforced anti-trust laws—cuts values, jobs and freedom for that sovereign public majority which continues to condone what is being thereby done to the public.

The overly indulgent administration of labor laws and of other laws affecting union conduct—and the granting of immunities which unions enjoy to the exclusion of all others in our society—continue to be carried on by the police, the courts and other national, state and local agencies charged with dealing out even-handed justice. Where such does not immediately destroy, it puts under continued and meaningful threat the persons and savings of most all that sovereign majority which itself permits these anti-social practices. Meanwhile, that majority's daily consumer values, worker jobs and quality of life are the poorer.

The National Labor Relations Board continues to favor the unions by needlessly extending the scope of bargainable matters and, in the process, persists in putting obstacles in the way of management's ability to accomplish technological progress and otherwise increase efficiency in consumer and worker interest—while continuing to give union officials more and more freedom to impede productivity inexcusably and interfere with the attainment of good values, attractive jobs and an improved quality of life.

When strikes occur, public opinion has been previously conditioned to tolerate gang picketing which illegally denies entrance to jobs and property, violent attacks which are made or meaningfully threatened to the persons and families of members and non-members alike, and property destruction not only to investors' savings but also to the cars and homes of members and non-members. Such flagrant law-breaking against the public is strangely endured as somehow both necessary and permissible for the successful pursuit of presumed gains for some, and are not only to be expected but suffered without recourse to enforcement of the applicable laws which would be instantly invoked for the same acts if done by law-breakers not union-connected. Here again, the public majority's misled permissiveness is resulting not only in periodic damage in big chunks but in daily loss of consumer values, worker jobs and quality of life.

Laws—or the NLRB interpretations of them —imperil the employer's right to free speech, thus denying employees and the rest of the public that full access to the facts on which to base their decisions in their own interests.

The NLRB and courts have failed to differentiate between the interests of union officials and the interests of union members. This favors unions being run to suit the political needs of the union officials in contrast to the economic and working-condition interests of the members. It inescapably reduces consumer values, worker jobs, and the quality of life.

Both government action and interim public opinion pressure have neglected to hold unions accountable for carrying out the obligations which inescapably accompany such opportunities as the public has given them. They should strive to aid the competitive ability and other progress of the companies which are trying to supply jobs to the union members represented through supplying attractive values to customers. They should live up to negotiated settlements and other arrangements in the same reliable and honorable way that is rightly expected of management. The failure of union conduct to be properly disciplined by the public majority, as well as by the union member majority, is resulting in consumer values, worker jobs and the quality of life being much the poorer.

Congress has been understandably resistant to passing the clearly needed reforms despite public opinion polls which consistently show that a majority of people, including a majority of union members, believe that unions now have too much power and would support the enactment of the corrective legislation needed to eliminate or at least minimize this current excess of power. Congress continues resistant and inactive—despite all this evidence as to the *state* of public opinion—simply because the public majority is not as *actively and even as threateningly* demanding as are the union political representatives whom the Congressmen see every day and who are in position to give the determining financial and vote-delivering re-election aid as long as the majority only supinely *prefers* the needed change and does not rouse itself to *demand* that change as the price of reelection.

Meanwhile, the public majority—and union membership majorities—need both to understand what now typically goes on at the actual bargaining and to demand that such be changed to meet the proper economic and moral criteria.

Bargaining—if it is to serve its intended purpose of arriving at equity for all concerned—must be recognized as affecting not only employees and investors but also consumers, suppliers and the rest of the involved public.

Since so much is at stake for so many, collective bargaining needs to be a sober and unemotional process of sincere cooperation in the competent search for that settlement which is the nearest possible in human affairs to what is in the balanced best interests of all concerned.

No matter how the market price of labor has been distorted by prior union, government or other action, the objective of the search must be to identify that market price and then settle on it—else the result will be either inflation or unemployment.

How often in my own experience years back did I listen to the characteristic demands for still "more" with the chilling fact before me that just one extra penny per hour above the market would mean either that an extra $5,000,000 per year above the market would have to be collected from our customers or that—to save the rest of the jobs—a way would have to be found for the jobs of 1000 of our employees to be eliminated with consequent damage not only to the 1000 families but to the merchants, schools, churches and homes of the communities involved!

Every union negotiator and every management negotiator should—and can—come to the bargaining table with his honestly stated position, public and private, being based on pretty accurate knowledge of what is the market and thus what will permit goods to flow and jobs to function. Any differences will then be so minor as to be easily adjusted. If either of the negotiators is not competent and diligent enough to meet this test, he should be replaced—just as in the case of those who fail substantially in prejudging product market prices.

In contrast to this is the currently too prevalent practice of the employer being forced to make his initial offer at a level he knows to be way below what he should and will settle for later, and then allowing the union negotiators to appear to be dragging him unwillingly up to the much higher settlement which is about what he had in mind all the time.

This reflects the false idea that collective bargaining must necessarily be some game of wits, or contest of skills—or battle between enemies—where both equity and "face" must finally be served through the union negotiators emerging as clearly the victors by so substantial a margin as to be politically satisfactory to them.

What the N.L.R.B. practically decrees is that there has been "refusal to bargain" unless the employer has raised his initial offer (no matter how good) by enough to satisfy the political needs of the union officials. And I recently heard a highly paid consultant tell a large business audience it would be foolish not to take advantage of the fact that they could settle for less pay increase if they made their successive offers in a way that let the union officials have an obvious victory.

Collective bargaining too vitally affects too many people for it to be prostituted by the uneconomic and immoral foolishness now prevalent. It is up to the public majority to see that its representatives in unions, business and government make the long needed change.

Summary

In short, the task of the public majority right now is to evaluate anew the overgrown economic and political power of the unions, which stems basically from the unregulated monopoly, the enormous income usable politically, and the privileged violence.

This basic power is implemented by further unwise laws, by the administration of those bad laws in ways even more unwise, by the immunity from obeying the good laws applicable, and by the continued positive or passive majority public opinion support of what is going on.

It is to be hoped that such a fresh assessment will result in public majority demand for desirable corrections in the laws and their administration. Most representatives in government and unions will certainly be ready —and some probably very eager—to make the required changes once they are convinced to do so is "good politics" with a safe majority of the public.

Specific recommendations are being developed and issued by The Labor Law Reform Study Group and by other responsible groups and individuals for the repeal or revision of individual federal and state laws in the public interest.

Publications, associations, companies and individual

thought-leaders should meet their obligation to aid in the distribution of proper recommendations to, and in their being understood by, all the voters within the span of possible contact by these sources of helpful influence.

Then the individual citizen, in his own interest, needs to do two things: (1) write his views and urgent instructions to his legislative representatives about needed law changes, and (2) meanwhile be telling and writing his union representatives, his law enforcement representatives—and his newspapers, broadcasters, teachers and clergymen—that he demands the help of them all in putting an end to privileged coercion.

In all this the proper objective of the public majority will be not to eliminate unions where wanted but to bring them up to the constructive usefulness they were originally intended to supply.

Chapter VI

THE THOUGHT-LEADER REQUIREMENT

The public majority cannot expect much, if any, initial help from the sources which would, in other circumstances, be expected to provide the corrective information and guidance now needed.

Despite some outstanding exceptions already—and hopefully more to come—these will not be nearly enough to get the required job under way.

Most political representatives in unions and government just cannot risk losing votes by disagreeing with a current consensus before that consensus has been changed to another which is safely "good politics" to follow.

Most press and air-wave communicators cannot be expected either to risk shut down or other damage through telling the whole truth about the cost to the public of union absuses in their shops—or meanwhile, to risk killing off advertising revenue by driving off readers and listeners with unpleasant disillusionment of the majority as to its false expectations of something-for-nothing—*until* others have accomplished enough change in public majority understanding to make it safely "good publishing" and "good broadcasting" to join in helping with the rest of the corrective teaching needed.

Most educators cannot be expected to risk their jobs and their futures by offending powerfully placed people through disillusioning the students—about the untruths they may have, with the best of intentions, been taught at home and even in church, as well as through the other information channels—*until* others have pioneered enough corrective teaching to make doing so be safely "good education" so far as parents, school boards, fellow faculty members, union officials, legislative appropriators, and rich contributors with guilt-complexes are concerned.

Most national, state and local business associations already advocate somewhat more corrective action than their members are willing or equipped to carry out. But they cannot get very much ahead of what the majority of the members is ready to approve, since there is such a surprisingly wide spectrum of member opinion as to what corrective responsibility the individual association should assume, and since a staff is thus usually rather narrowly limited as to what is "good association" work in its particular case. Yet there are outstanding examples of individual association executives who do manage to pioneer corrective materials and methods and to bring some proportion of the membership along in a corrective program.

Most successful businesses of medium and large size —and especially the most successful and thus the most politically conspicuous and headline-vulnerable—cannot be expected to forget that they are artificial beings created by public permission and operating at the pleasure of the public which pays the operating bill. They hence can only be expected to do what is "good business" by doing about as the public rightly or wrongly demands. Yet there is, even within this convenient concept, considerable leeway promptly, easily and *safely* to help the public majority stop what it is doing to itself through what it is directly and indirectly doing to business as well as doing through other even more far-reaching activities.

Meanwhile, the point is that most of those who are considered the public majority's present thought-leaders are, in this matter, more followers than leaders. They are not only parties to the debilitating current consensus but also not about to *initiate* any change in course.

So the public majority needs a new set of thought-leaders. For it is not, on its own, going to be able to acquire the new competency which it does not yet even appreciate it needs in its increasingly complicated situation. And the vast majority of thought-leaders now in place will not function in the needed way in the beginning.

Hence the new breed of real thought-leaders will have to be largely self-appointed, self-directed, and self-propelled. They are needed at every level from bottom to top in our society.

Where are they going to come from? They will have to be grown!

Some are already full grown and at work. Happily, still more are sprouting without help.

But I believe it is obvious that business is the only one of the public's agencies which now combines its own pressing need and obligation with an unrestricted opportunity to sow the seed needed to grow *enough* of these leaders in the public interest while going on about its other regular duties in the fields now being cultivated.

First, about 10% of the employees of every business are accepted inside the company and out in the community as thought-leaders in technological, financial and commercial matters. These are the managers at every level, including foremen, the professional specialists such as engineers, accountants, salesmen, production and personnel people, the secretaries, receptionists, service men and others whose obvious interest and whose specialized training and experience give them the authority of knowledge. These citizens are the potential —and can be made the actual—corrective thought-leaders for the better understanding of business intentions, practices and results in general and of the current issues in particular. All most of them require is adequate access to the information needed for transmission to others.

Second, business has intimate *written* contact with individuals in most every household every week and again every month and meanwhile in about half the households every quarter. This written opportunity can be embraced easily, promptly and with practically no expense by including a printed or even mimeographed message of about three hundred words in an envelope with each weekly pay check, each monthly statement and each quarterly dividend as will be discussed in more detail later.

Despite the apparently limitless complexity and scope of the problem, the needed corrective information is readily available in brief, palatable form for those who do not choose to write their own.

Beginning on page 139 ahead, there are some examples of the varied ways in which the corrective facts can be easily combined with current news significance and fitted to the recipient's own immediate interest—and need for action—as worker, consumer or saver.

The basic correction work which business can safely do even in the present circumstances—and which owners and managers need to do in their own interest just as much as in the interest of others—does not involve government or unions as such but has to do with where consumer values and worker jobs come from and how both can be made better through the proper operation of a business where all concerned believe they have reason to cooperate—and do cooperate—toward the good ends of that business.

It is to be noted that the examples from page 139 through 178 do not even once mention the words "union" or "Republican" or "Democrat". Any company could spend a year on corrective information of only this type—and even lifted largely from just Chapters 3 and 4—in an effort to accomplish the improvement in cooperation and productivity needed in employee and other public interest.

Any mention of disagreement with union representatives would be made only in the case of some unexpected and acute need. But even then it would likely do no good, unless the management at all levels had already met the two prior requirements involved.

The first of these is to have corrected any "brute" or other adverse impression even of disinterest. This has to have been accomplished through deserving and winning the confidence of employees and neighbors that management is genuinely *trying* in their behalf. It has to have been proved to them by looks, actions, and results that management from bottom to top has the human considerations up front and both *wants and intends*— within the opportunities offered and limitations imposed by customers—to have procedures and results come as close as possible to what employees and neighbors would like.

The second of these is the requirement to have debunked any crook, exploiter or other conflict-of-interest impression and to have contributed week by week to the gradual growth in sound economic understanding of jobs, values and business. This will have provided the necessary background of knowledge and the equally necessary recognition that management can and does talk equitable economic sense from the employee and community standpoint.

If management has delayed until a strike looms—or until otherwise it is suddenly imperative to disagree with the principle or logic involved in union proposals or actions—any effort then at helpful information will at once be emotionally rejected. This is for the simple reason that the "prior homework" required in the emotional and economic areas has not been done patiently and thoroughly enough over a long enough period. Management has not equipped employees and other public to judge the current discussion with calmness and sophistication against the background of already familiar principles. Management has likewise failed to qualify itself so that its further offerings of facts and recommendations in the specific situation will fit in with an already established belief that it makes mutually rewarding proposals and does such things ably and sincerely in trying to serve the balanced best interests of all concerned.

In short, when trouble comes, it is then too late to try to supply the corrections needed. It is unfair to employees—as well as to others—to have waited. Where union and allied agencies are continuing to make a seemingly believed case for the employer's bad intentions and bad economics—or where the union forces are silent because their case is already in—it is vitally necessary to do daily the corrective job needed in employee and other public interest. And remember that the damage done to productivity, values and employment by misinformation and misconceived prejudices does not occur just periodically at the time some union trouble surfaces but goes on all day long every day.

The businessman has fallen to his now so dangerous state of public discredit, disapproval and cooperation resistance because—despite his obvious need, obligation and wide-open opportunity to do so—he has not met the steadily mounting requirement to explain the good which private business does for the many and to debunk—through obviously deserving to do so—the basic brute, crook and exploiter charges which too many employees, consumers and even savers believe and on which they and their political representatives act to the detriment of those same employees, consumers and savers.

Employees are being successfully taught to regard their interests as directly opposed to those of management. Their cooperation in more output-per-man-and-his-machine—and in eliminating make-work, feather-bedding and other waste—is not admitted to be precisely the means needed to get better values through to the consumer. Instead, it is misrepresented as against the interest of everyone but the owners since, it is claimed, all this improvement only helps further swell profits which are already dishonestly swollen. It has been estimated—and proved in many instances—that this unwise opposition cuts efficiency by a minimum of 20% in most businesses.*

Employees, consumers and even too many savers are being successfully persuaded that business greed, power and profit are what cause inflation and unemployment, and that business—despite inability to recover the costs in prices—should be forced to keep the unneeded employees and supply jobs to the unemployed, all at pay which both compensates for inflation and meets the unrealistic expectations for the higher level of living desired without higher output to match.

If employees and the others concerned are not quickly helped to learn the facts about inflation and unemployment, businesses will increasingly fail to get prices which cover costs and will thus increasingly find it impossible to supply jobs at all.

---

* See Chapters 6 and 11 of Truth About Boulwarism.

Just as importantly complicating the business cost-price dilemma is the heedless drive by employees, customers and even savers to have government supply vast services for which these same employees, consumers and savers refuse to pay directly and must be charged the cost through the tax of inflation hidden in business costs and hence in higher consumer prices. The result will be more inflation, or fewer jobs, or both, and be blamed on business.

The damaging attacks are made under various guises on private business by its ideological competitors not only in personal contact but on the air, in the press, in school and college courses, and even in much of what is put forward with the best of intentions in our churches and unthinkingly accepted by too many as the word of God.

Any such charges about a business and its management, if put forward by a *commercial* competitor, would have been met fully and forthrightly in public as well as in the courts. In the face of such character assassination by his *ideological* competitors, however, the businessman has too generally heeded the unrealistic and otherwise bad advice that he still try to "maintain a low profile". But what he has thus succeeded in doing is only to maintain so highly conspicuous a silence as to appear to confess guilt as charged.

The inevitably resulting damage is all around us in the crisis we see climaxing now not only for business but for the public's interests elsewhere in our society. Not only every owner and manager—but also every other conscientious citizen in his various roles—needs to serve his own interest by promptly doing all he can to get capable to help his fellow citizen to identify the bad arithmetic and bad morals of the current false teaching and resulting false expectations, and thus to help all

124

concerned get on the track toward the truly rewarding achievements still open to us as a people.

Unless people learn the facts about business—and learn especially *how they must help business serve them* —there is not only going to be no profit to maintain values and jobs but there is also too likely to be no free enterprise, no private property and no freedom.

When faced with anywhere near such a cost or peril from a massive water leak, or from a mounting fire hazard, or from a vicious competitor publicly lying or even joyfully telling the truth—or from an excited public demanding pollution be stopped regardless of cost— owners and managers quickly learn how to meet the situation and go promptly at making whatever investment in study and funds is necessary to head off or cure the actual condition or the false impression.

Yet in this ideological war—where only words are doing the major damage and where the proper words, *properly backed,* can produce the major remedy—owners and managers keep needlessly resigning themselves to inactivity, even though such neglect is causing horrendous losses to workers, consumers, savers and communities. Researchers attribute many reasons for this, such as:

1. It's not our business. We are not politicians. We are not our workers' or our country's keeper. Our job is to turn out goods and services.
2. It's no use. People are too disinterested, other than being intrigued with promises of an easy way out.
3. It's too late. Business has been licked, and the public has been had. We should subside and simply do the best we can within what is permitted.

4. It's too dangerous. And we are not equipped for such an activity anyway.
5. We are successful by past standards—and thus have been smarter than most of our competitors. We hope to survive and even get rich regardless of rules that may liquidate most others.
6. It's the public that is doing this. If the public wants government, unions and business run this way, who are we to stick our necks out and take on the thankless job of disillusioning people about cherished fallacies they have been taught by leaders they blindly trust.

Yet the stakes were never so breath-taking. And it would seem the opportunity of the businessman—and his corresponding obligation to himself as well to as others—were never before anything like so great.

For the realities now facing business dictate that—unless a tremendous improvement in public understanding is accomplished over a very short period—the public's representatives will continue to be forced or permitted to do what will look properly corrective but is actually further damaging to their inadequately informed constituents.

This is because these constituents will be continuing in about the same misinformed and unsophisticated state which has brought on our current difficulty.

This will, in turn, be because the public majority—which determines both elections and the net thrust of public opinion between elections—will not have received the needed help promptly from those who should be the sources of corrective guidance, such as teachers, editors, broadcasters, clergymen, entertainers, the majority of other presently active thought-leaders, and that vast majority of businessmen who continue on the too characteristic course of silence on controversial public issues even when those issues are vitally business-connected.

Happily, there are many outstanding exceptions among all these potentially helpful folks, but they are still far too few. Most of them—for reasons they believe adequate—will not take the lead in debunking that big portion of "the current consensus" whose pursuit in the name of helping, is actually damaging consumers, earners, savers and seekers after the better material and non-material life generally.

As is understandably true of most politicians, most of these other leaders with the corrective potential will come along only after their doing so has become safely "good politics" with the majority of their particular segment of the public.

Yet, enough sufficiently able and alarmed citizens simply must now boldly and promptly take the lead, if it is going to be possible for government and business to be instructed or permitted by the public majority to attack constructively our critical current problems.

My own earnest hope is that businessmen all across the country will take this lead. In fact, I believe they are the only ones left available to do it, and that, unless they do it, it will not be done.

To do so will be in their own urgent interest as well as the public interest. For I reluctantly conclude that neither private business and its obvious usefulness— nor the incentives, free choice, private ownership and responsive limited government we have enjoyed—can survive for long now unless we citizens in the majority are helped to have a sounder economic understanding, a more rewarding moral motivation and a more adequate political sophistication.

The public majority got us into our present fix—or let us get into it—and only the public majority can get us out of it. For democracy, even when most effective, is still only a device for responding to the majority's good or bad judgment, and any success depends on the ability and willingness of the more soundly informed citizens to convince the majority to change course constructively when things get going wrong.

It is true that such corrective work has not been considered a part of the manager's job. As already indicated, he has not been taught that it is by his predecessors, his superiors, his professional management consultants, his business press, or his graduate or undergraduate business schools.

But the situation is now so urgent for everybody involved with business—that is, for the consumers, employees, suppliers, investors, tax-collectors and neighboring homeowners—that the individual manager simply must face two immediate requirements: first, to fix any deficiencies about which public dissatisfaction with his business is warranted. Second, to correct the still mounting misunderstanding about the rest.

Fortunately, in doing just this second, he will have to be doing the whole correction—about inflation, unemployment, productivity and profit—needed by that part of the public majority which is within the span of his possible reach.

And despite the normally expected channels for corrective education of this kind being closed, the businessman has no problem. As already indicated, the needed corrective information is available from many sources in palatable form. *All he has to do as a starter is to put these brief and inexpensive stuffers in the envelopes he is alreading sending out every week, month and quarter.*

Obviously the course of history could be changed in ninety days if all businessmen would step up to this opportunity. But the individual businessman need not and should not wait for others. He will furnish a compelling example to others—and meanwhile will *immediately* benefit the employees, customers and savers involved in his own business—when he starts to:

1. Insert stuffers with the pay checks each week to *his part* of the nation's 80,000,000 non-government employees—all of whom desperately need the real story on inflation, unemployment, productivity, and profit in order for them to think and act more soundly in their own interests.*
2. Insert stuffers *with his part* of the hundreds of million monthly statements going to customers of retailers, manufacturers, doctors, banks, telephone companies, electric and gas companies, etc.—all of which customers are vitally interested in prices and should activate themselves properly in their own interests.
3. Insert stuffers *with his part* of the 40,000,000 quarterly dividend checks going to people who too little realize that it is not business managers, but they the business owners, who are under lethal attack and who need selfishly, as well as patriotically, to get busy knowing and telling the correct story of the great good done for all by investment and profit.

Fortunately, there is no need to get into personalities and attack the sources of the misconceptions which have done us in. All that is required is to go after the so obviously bad arithmetic and bad morals involved in the present futile quest for something-for-nothing through gang force imposed at the ballot box, the bargaining table, or the scene of privileged violence.

---

* Where pay envelopes are not used, there are obviously many other means of having the corrective message attached to or accompany the paycheck.

Despite the existing limitations already noted, the business associations and the business press can be of very substantial help while still not getting too far ahead of their members and readers they are trying to bring along toward meeting their job and personal responsibilities more capably and actively.

The business press—at each of the national, state, local and individual industry levels—can continuously from here on publish suggestions to their readers in the form of ready-made corrective employee, customer and stockholder articles which—"as is" or revised to apply to the individual company—can be used as envelope stuffers or as items included in company publications going to these three groups. They can not only publish their own suggested copy in each issue but also run a clearing house for the better of the examples which readers have been encouraged to send in showing how they have written their own articles or have modified those supplied.

Likewise—and maybe even more importantly—the national, state and local business associations can generate articles of their own within whatever is their current policy, and then offer these to their membership along with the best they get from elsewhere.

The local association in particular has now a new opportunity for usefulness through cooperating with—or even supplying the leadership for—some few or many of its members who initiate what they hope will become a "saturation" program of community-wide corrective teaching such as is at this writing just getting under way at Rockford, Illinois. The idea of the several businessmen who initiated this program is simply to practice what they preach in their own businesses—while trying to persuade most all the other businesses in town to join progressively *one by one* in doing the same until practically every employee in the community gets a corrective message every week, every local consumer gets several every month, and every local stockholder gets several every quarter.

Highly important to keep in mind, however, is that the individual businessman cannot afford to delay the start until even such a simple program may have become association-wide policy or until a smaller independent group should decide to go ahead. Either might take too long—and might never come about—for reasons noted earlier.

The lone businessman needs to go ahead on his own if he does not get immediate company, and even if the local association executive is in no position informally to help the one employer do what the latter independently wants to do. The rewards to the lone business in increased productivity and in other cooperation are far more than adequate compensation for the little extra study and modest investment required. The procedures to follow could be as easy as these:

1.

The first step—as already indicated—is simply to start sending the corrective messages with the weekly pay checks, monthly statements and quarterly dividends. This not only will supply the recipients with information helpful to their own attitudes and acts in and out of the business but also will put lots of them to work on others less well-informed.

The recently used examples shown in the back of the book can be revised to suit or many can even be used about "as is". Many of them were obviously drawn from prior publications of mine—as well as from the front of this book which was in preparation at the time and which could be a still further source. And there are twenty-one pages of illustrated suggestions in "The Truth About Boulwarism". Other and better suggested copy from national and local associations such as from the Chamber of Commerce and from NAM's special service for company publications—and from business publications and individual companies—are already amply available and will surely become increasingly so. Further excellent material can be drawn from the sources cited in sections ahead.

And a new source is Hillsdale College, Hillsdale, Michigan, 49242. A panel of distinguished economists from outside is joining with the school's own economics teachers to produce short corrective articles which relate the applicable economic principles to current public controversies and to the very immediate problems and worries of employees, of consumers and of the owners of business securities and other private property. These will be suitable for columns in daily newspapers and house organs as well as to accompany weekly pay checks, monthly statements and quarterly dividends.

But messages generated within a local business— with some genuine immediate reason for them—are always the best. Each business can profitably strive toward that. The requirement is simply that the message be of timely, acute and helpful interest in connection with some problem or issue which involves all concerned there. Meanwhile, the use of messages lifted from elsewhere will be doing a lot of good in the given company and its community.

2.

The next step is to identify individually the employees making up that approximately 10% who are the present technological, financial and commercial thought-leaders and whose brains, interest and standing make them *potentially* the corrective thought-leaders needed in the ideological field.

Then supply a copy of this book to each of them*— being sure each one is handed personally to the employee by his immediate superior who can in his own words say something to this effect:

> "I think we each in our position have a new and urgent duty as corrective thought-leaders in our jobs and with our associates outside."
>
> "I have read this book on what the responsible business and community leader needs to know and do in his own and the common interest about job-connected, business-connected and community-connected problems in economics, morals and non-partisan politics."
>
> "I would like you to read it in the next week, and then we will discuss it. While you are reading it, I hope you will be asking yourself this question:
>
> Do I, or don't I, have personally just as great an *obligation* to myself, my associates, my family and my neighbors as I have *opportunity* for gaining and imparting now needed information, sophistication and guidance by reason of my superior native ability, my superior attainments, and my access to superior information?"

---

* This recommendation may need to be viewed in this dual light. (1) As the Preface states, I take no compensation at all from this book and hence hope I may be spared any suspicion of self-serving in making this recommendation and (2) At the price of $1.35, less applicable quantity discount, the cost of giving this book to all the 10%—for them, their families and neighbors to read on their own time for their own good—is less than the company cost would be for the recipient to attend even one 5 minute meeting to hear just a little of what is in the book— LRB

The next step a week later—and progressively downward from the top—is to have each manager meet with those of the 10% directly responsible to him. He can restate his conviction as to the new need to help all within their possible span of influence to think and act more in their own interest at work and away from work and—in the process—to achieve more, better and steadier jobs through increased cooperation in accomplishing more attractive values.

He can then check their interest and try to reinforce the interest of the as yet lukewarm ones. But he will not then—or later—get uniform acceptance of, devotion to or excellence in the new leadership. So he must not wait, but send them out with the individuals varying in what they privately intend to do.

Fortunately, most people want to help others and would like to feel they are deservedly accepted as an authority having superior information of help about questions bothering others. And the power of the example by some—plus just getting used to the idea—will help greatly in bringing many of the others along.

The manager at any upper level may find it helpful or even necessary to remind his associates that—while this corrective thought-leadership program will take no appreciable investment in company money—it admittedly will not only call for acquiring some addition to the usual managerial equipment in the form of new knowledge and of new ready facility in the use of that knowledge, but will also oblige a somewhat altered habit or sequence of managerial action. This is because of the now mounting significance—and new profit importance—of these two hard facts of business right now:

The first is the already familiar fact that—to have the opportunity to be otherwise successful in supplying attractive values and jobs, a company must first achieve *technological, financial and commerical* skills of such excellence that they can do *their part*—though *not all*—toward offering values attractive enough to bring in sales at that profit which warrants the risk and use of the savings required and makes those savings available internally or through outsiders.

The second hard fact and suddenly now the determining one is that, over and beyond the foregoing first one, the company's final success or failure as to costs, profit and even survival has come more and more to depend—and will even more so from hereon—on the degree of cooperation or non-cooperation it can *both earn and get* from the various individuals involved as a result of their corrected economic, moral and political orientation about business and about how the level of living is actually raised.

4.

The next step is to be sure each manager gets into genuine two-way communication alone with each one of his direct charges in the 10% in order to uncover and then really clear up any hidden dissatisfactions. This should, of course, have been and be done regularly whether or not there is any new or revised program.

But this is a good excuse to renew the emphasis on finding out in each individual case what are rightly or wrongly considered management's sins of commission and omission, its actual and fancied defects, and what are the individual's other meaningful likes and dislikes, approvals and disapprovals, trusts and distrusts, expectations and disappointments, right down to his attitude about productivity, profit and the fairness of his own pay.*

---

* See the Chapter on the "The Manager's Own Nine Point Job' in The Truth About Boulwarism."

There is no point to go on not knowing of things that ought to be fixed and others that ought to be explained to the individual's satisfaction—much less trying to send someone out to convert others who is not himself a true believer.

5.

Then to keep the oral communication equipment of the 10% up to date, constantly amplified and refreshed—and to stimulate the written communicators with current material—it will usually be advisable to supply weekly a separate publication to all the 10%, even though it be as simple as four mimeographed pages. In addition, it will be highly desirable to supply as many as possible of the 10% at each location *daily* with significant Wall Street Journal editorials and with the mimeographed daily Victor Riesel report on labor and related political developments, *weekly* with helpful material drawn from Industry Week and association publications, *monthly* with a rotated *Freeman Magazine,* and periodically with resource books such as "Man vs The Welfare State" by Henry Hazlitt (Arlington House) and "Dividing the Wealth" by Dr. Howard E. Kirschner (Devin-Adair).

Incidentally, the Victor Riesel report is recommended because it has been found invaluable as both a sophisticating agent and an objective reminder of the little known extent and effectiveness with which labor union power is constantly exercised as the determining force over governments and the economies here and abroad. This daily report is available through writing Victor Riesel, Suite 1906, 30 E. 46th Street, New York, N.Y., 10017.

OTHER THOUGHT-LEADERS

Despite the foregoing emphasis on the opportunities and obligations of the 10% in business to become corrective thought-leaders in and out of business, the fact must not be overlooked that the same opportunity and obligation is inherent in every other individual who is not plugging a partisan political position and has earned, or can earn, a span of influence great or small.

Included are those—beyond the top 10% in business—who are now either formal or informal thought-leaders on other questions at home, school, church circle, civic meeting, card club, service club luncheon, bowling alley, golf course or around the stove at the country store.

One figure to keep in mind is our over 50,000,000 adult women. A number of those have responsible positions in business, teaching, government and elsewhere. But there simply must, in every community and even in every local neighborhood, be a still high proportion of the top 10%—as to their financial, mental, energy and spare-time resources—who do not believe their ability and desire for usefulness can ever be satisfied by the activities now customarily open to them. Many of these women will undoubtedly welcome an introduction to a new and challenging opportunity to make a worthwhile contribution in the area of their friends' greatest immediate concern and long-term well being.

What is needed in every neighborhood, club or other group is simply a self-starting, self-appointed leader—man or woman—who will embrace the evident opportunity and obligation in the contacts available to him or her.

To The Reader:

You must be a daily witness to about 10% of the men and women in your office, plant, store, bank, church, club and neighborhood supplying accepted thought-leadership in one or more areas important to the other 90%.

I hope you feel this little book would help most of these leaders supply their followers with some of the new guidance now needed on the worker-connected, consumer-connected and saver-connected questions uppermost today.

If so, I hope you will want to order a copy for many or all of them in response to the publisher's offer below.

Lemuel R. Boulware

Chapter VII

On the following pages are the examples mentioned earlier.

These are only random illustrations of the kind of needed corrective information now beginning to be widely—although not yet widely enough—supplied by associations, foundations, companies and individual writers for use, "as is" or revised, in helpful non-partisan communications to employees, consumers, property owners, and voters.

Some of them are obviously tied in with the particular wage stabilization problems the country faced in the winter of 1971-72. These illustrate how the needed corrective economics and other facts can be linked to specific problems of currently most vital concern to workers, consumers and savers.

There are also some which were lifted from the foregoing text as it was being prepared for the classroom. These illustrate how simple it would be in the future to lift these and other parts of the text in helping to supply pertinent discussion of specific problems then uppermost in the news and in public concern.

Pages 140 through 178 are examples in which unions are not mentioned. From 179 on, they are mentioned.

Many of the originals of the following contained pertinent graphic illustrations which have nevertheless been omitted in the interests of space.

COULD YOU EQUIP YOUR JOB?

Sometime ago it was figured that if productivity continued to increase by 3% a year, it would be possible by 1990 to get the same output in a 20-hour week or to be able to retire at 38 if a 40-hour week were worked.

Back there in 1967, the big part of U.S. production done by machinery required an average investment of $19,811 for each employee to be able to do his part and draw his pay.

The petroleum industry had the highest investment —$136,178. per employee. Tobacco had $43,276., motor vehicles had $39,814., chemicals had $34,850., primary metals $27,670., and paper $20,878. per employee.

But despite these surprising figures, the 20-hour week —or the retirement at 38 with the same level of living as now—is having to be pushed much past 1990.

One reason is that the required investment per employee is not only much higher now but headed still higher. This is not only due to the higher cost of equipment because of inflation and low productivity but is due also to the less than full application of skill, care and effort in the use of improved equipment.

Another reason is that the now required work on pollution and environment correction—which work is unproductive of either producer or consumer goods—must be done by workers who are fed, clothed, housed, educated and entertained by that remainder of the work force who must turn out enough producer and consumer goods and services both for themselves and for the new army of workers not productively engaged.

Under these circumstances, that worker who can fully finance his own job is going to be rarer than ever.

And it is going to take more encouragement than ever for others to be able to save and risk enough investment to equip the worker to maintain his own high level of living while supplying an equally high one to those not producing.

OUR CRISIS OF FALSE EXPECTATIONS

We as a people are in a crisis such as we have never before faced. It stems from false expectations grown to heroic proportions.

Too few of us understand inflation, unemployment, productivity and profit. As a result, too many of us have been misled into demanding and expecting that our take will be much greater than is our contribution to what is available to take.

We want too much too soon too largely from someone else. We have come to believe that government or business or others can and will somehow supply the difference now between what we want and what we individually produce.

But workers really *work for themselves—through* their employer. For workers—as consumers—pay most all the expenses of any business which long survives. These expenses—including all wages, taxes and even charity—are paid in current consumer prices, or in delayed progress in future values, or in both.

And workers—as tax-paying consumers—also supply all the money which government spends. This money is taken in visible direct taxes, or in taxes which government first collects from business and then makes business hide in higher consumer prices, or in the "tax of inflation" which government collects from consumers through dishonorably counterfeiting under the pleasant name of "monitizing debt."

We only have what we produce. There is just no way —directly or through any agency—to get something-for-nothing. Not only is it economically impossible to do so, but it is also immoral even to try.

What seems most needed right now is for the majority of us to gain the economic information, the moral alertness and the political sophistication needed to enable us to distinguish between the always silly something-for-nothing proposal and the truly constructive procedure toward a realizable goal.

WAGES STILL RISING
FASTER THAN PRICES!

Most of us may feel that prices are rising faster than pay. But, if so, we are wrong.

Ever since last July—the month before the freeze —average non-farm pay rates have increased twice as fast as consumer prices. Retail wages have gone up two times as fast, manufacturing pay rates three times as fast as consumer prices. Retail wages have gone up 2½ as fast, and contract construction wages (even from their high base) about three times as fast as the consumer price index.

In fact, with the exception of some war months, wage rates have risen about twice as fast as prices in every year of this entire century. The difference has, of course, been made up by productivity increases resulting somewhat from increased skill, care and effort but mostly from increased investment in improved equipment.

The basic cause of so many of us being misled about this is threefold. First, except for a short period around 1952 or 1953, our government has neglected to show both the wage and price change in the same monthly release. Second, the press and broadcasters have failed to dig up the related wage change to include with their reports of price change. Third, those with a political interest in creating a false impression have thus been given a free hand.

Perhaps contributing to the ease of our being misled is that most of us tend to lose sight of the size of our annual or other pay rise and are thus disproportionately distressed at seeming always to find each successive purchase priced higher than the last.

But prices are not actually going up as fast as wages even now. And this is all the more remarkable because —whenever an effort is made suddenly to stabilize wages and prices—there is inevitably a lot of recent wage increases which have already been paid but are still back up the pipe line. They have already gone into the costs of raw materials and goods in process but will not show up until later in the costs and prices of finished goods.

We may not have all we want—and we may not be progressing toward that as fast as we would like—but it is not because prices are outstripping wage rates.

Inflation—
A LOOK IN THE MIRROR

Most of us are now deeply concerned about who and what are causing our inflation, what will stop it, and who meanwhile should or does pay the cost of inflation. Here are some views, for what they are worth, to put alongside the many others you are getting on this controversial subject from all sides.

Inflation comes from our government believing it is politically necessary to create worthless extra money (and credit) for which there are no extra goods and services to match—and to do so for these two reasons:

1. To provide the money for the government to pay for those goods and services which the public majority wants or permits some or all of the public to receive at so-called "government expense". The public majority loosely assumes the money is going to come from somewhere else, and would flatly refuse to pay the cost visibly or knowingly. Thus our government—believing it politically necessary to at least *appear* to be doing what its constituents demand or allow—is forced by the public to resort to the deceitful process of collecting the cost from that same unsuspecting public through the tax of inflation hidden in higher consumer prices.

2. To pump out added worthless cash—which increases the number and cuts the value of all our dollars—so that consumers will have enough cheapened dollars to buy at the higher consumer prices now necessitated by the *total* of the artificially higher pay—that is, the total of the higher wages *and higher cost-of-living allowances*—which higher total is imposed in the absence of higher output to match, would only kill or reduce jobs if money is left at its old value, and is in accordance with the pay practices demanded or permitted by the affected but unseeing consuming public itself. Thus what government is really doing is, first, to promote or sanction the unworkable pay increase and then promptly wipe out the expected buying-power increase in an attempt to mask or to delay temporarily the job-killing effect of such pay raises without correspondingly raised output.

To stop or minimize inflation, *both* No. 1 and No. 2 above must be stopped or minimized. And in connection with No. 2, it is this *total*—of *both* wage increases and cost-of-living allowance increases—which has to be tapered down to at most 3% a year for the country as a whole (to match the presumed or hoped-for productivity increase) if inflation is to be arrested.

It is to your interest to tell your representatives and fellow citizens—and to write Judge Boldt, Chairman of the Pay Board—how you feel about this, whatever that may be.

WITH FAIRNESS TO ALL—
and
PRIVILEGE TO NONE

Most of our fellow citizens have warmly welcomed the President's program to cut inflation to 2 to 3% by the end of 1972. To accomplish this, it has been made very clear that total employment cost increases must not *average* more than 5%, and that productivity must meanwhile be steadily and substantially improved.

This time—as in past impositions of restraints for the common good—most of us have been *initially* enthusiastic about the idea of controls. For things had obviously gone wrong, and we wanted any abuses stopped. But it is the rare one of us who does not assume that he should rightly go free of any restrictions and that it is only the others who need to be controlled.

Most of us are thus doubly shocked when we begin to appreciate not only that the controls apply to us too, but also that we have even been largely responsible for the controls being needed because of what we ourselves have unwisely done and what we have unwisely asked

145

or permitted our representatives to do. Nevertheless, we will quickly reconcile ourselves to paying our deserved share, while being very watchful that no one else goes undeservedly free.

The first test of such fairness is before the new Pay Board. The existing contracts in question, which were caught in the freeze, call for an *average total* — of increases in pay and increases in cost-of-living allowances —that exceeds the level required for stabilization. And in too many of these cases, the individual contracts call for a 10 to 15 percent additional cost in *wages* alone—*plus* the increased cost-of-living allowances.

The difference between such total new employment costs and the estimated 3% improvement in productivity must all go into still higher consumer prices, or still more unemployment, or entirely too much of both.

The contracts in question were imposed on very distressed employers at a time quite different from now. It was then expected that inflation was going to keep on accelerating, and that the resulting total employment cost—from both pay increases and increases in cost-of-living allowances—could continue to be recovered in large part from consumers in higher prices, with relatively little of the effect having to show up in increased unemployment.

The question before the Pay Board and the country now is: Will these existing contracts be permitted now to operate as arranged in a very different prior climate, or will they be brought—as new employment arrangements will have to be—in line with the nation's inflation-arresting and unemployment-correcting needs?

While this is an *economic* and *moral* question, it is having to be handled as a *political* matter. It will thus be helpful for you to let your representatives know how you feel—however that may be.

LET'S COOPERATE—
IN OUR OWN INTERESTS!

Phase II is with us—for good or bad. Each of us needs to do our level best to make it work to the greatest extent possible.

For if it does not work out fairly satisfactorily, Phase III and its successors will get progressively tougher on us all as earners, consumers and savers.

Furthermore, we will be less and less *free* to do as we please—at work, at the market, and elsewhere. We will be more and more *told* what to do. We will *not* like it.

The old excessive contracts permitted to continue, the new contracts at double or triple the intended ceiling, the inevitable exceptions for "catchups" and "inequities"—and the understandable feeling of the rest of us that we should likewise have not just the 5.5% but more—are all too likely to press inflation entirely too much above the 2% to 3% goal for 1972.

To help slow down this process—and help keep Phase III from being horrifyingly worse for everybody—we each need to do these three things in our own selfish interest as well as for the good of the country:

1. We need to recognize that consumers in the end pay most all the expenses of any business which long survives, and that these expenses are paid in higher prices at once, or in delayed future improvement in values, or in both.

2. We need thus to recognize that these concessions being made out of political necessity to the relatively few hundred thousand or million unionized workers are at the unfair expense—in prices, jobs and savings—of the rest of the 19 million union members, of the 65 million non-

147

union earners and, to only temporarily a lesser extent, of these very union members who are getting the presumably beneficial concession. We also need to recognize that those outside the work force—with or without savings—are also being very inequitably affected.

3. We each need to discuss these exceptions—and what we are now learning about the rest of our inflation, unemployment, productivity and profit problem—with all within our possible reach. This is to the end of our helping change it to "good politics" and "good business" for our representatives in government, unions and business to do what is genuinely right in our own and the common interest.

OUR COST OF GOVERNMENT
PER CITIZEN

In trying to meet and overcome the competition of foreign producers in our markets at home and abroad—and in trying to raise our level of living—we should stop putting up two roadblocks to our progress.

The first one—as most of us fortunately are beginning to recognize and try to do something about—is the roadblock we are raising in the form of publicly endorsed or tolerated pay rates artificially forced up to where they are, for instance, twice those of Germany and four times those of Japan.

We all, as consumers, pay these rates except in the case of that 10 or 15% of our particular purchases supplied from foreign sources. In addition, we as workers suffer unemployment by being priced out of both domestic and foreign markets which could otherwise take our output.

But we are now building up the second roadblock to unprecedented war or peacetime heights. And we do not seem yet to have even begun to suspect what we are thus doing to ourselves in the exact area of our currently greatest distress.

This second roadblock is the cost of government per person. It is the total of the taxes levied visibly as such, and of the tax of inflation hidden in consumer prices. It arises largely from government not only spending the all-time high of taxes collected visibly but also overspending those taxes by 25 to 40 billion dollars—up to another $200 per year per man, woman and child—which have to be collected from consumers in the hidden tax of inflation.

Needless to say, this total cost of government per person—from both the visible and hidden taxes—is the second big element not only in raising our cost of living but in making us uncompetitive with Germany and Japan, where the government cost per person is far below ours even when we deduct the Vietnam expense.

What we all need to do is to persuade our representatives that we understand this needlessly continued excess of government spending will more than wipe out any inflation-arresting and job-improving gains we can possibly accomplish through pay stabilization and increased productivity.

"COST-OF-LIVING" CATCH-UPS

It's mighty easy for each of us right now to feel that increases in our particular cost-of-living should be matched by an increase in what others pay us for what we do for them.

There are two reasons why we should correct this tendency in our own interest. The first is that we are ourselves each responsible for the rise in the cost of living because of what we do wrong ourselves along with what we instruct or allow our representatives to do wrong. We each deserve to and must pay the price and can't escape it.

The other reason is that a rise in the cost-of-living is simply the natural market forces collecting back the worthless extra money for which there are no matching goods. If such extra money—thus collected from consumers as the *tax of inflation*—is then *refunded* to them in a cost-of-living adjustment through their employer from the public, the inflationary process (of extra money with no extra goods to match) begins all over again. But this time it starts from a new higher base with its still more damaging effect in prices.

We want to remember that our inflation comes principally from our government printing extra money unmatched by extra output, and doing so for two purposes:

The first purpose is to manufacture the money to pay for the goods and services which government feels called on by the public to give to some or all citizens, but for which the public refuses to pay knowingly and hence has to pay through deceitful hidden tax of inflation. We need to tell our representatives to stop this and that we will support them at the polls for doing so.

The second purpose is—through further cheapening the dollar—to delay temporarily the unemployment which higher pay, unmatched with higher output, will inevitably cause when money is left at its former value. It is obvious, of course, that this practise not only adds to inflation but also wipes out the expected higher buying power of the unmatched pay increase.

Here too we need to tell our representatives we want them to change course—since we now realize not only that we cannot benefit by receiving a larger number of proportionately cheapened dollars, but also that our level of living can be raised only by our doing more for each other.

HOW MUCH ENVIRONMENT CLEAN-UP—
AT *YOUR* EXPENSE?

To judge from the political speeches and other press and airwave evidence, most all of us are now thought to demand instant cleanup of the man-made dirt and noise pollution in our air, water, streets, slums, highways, parks and remaining wilderness.

Of course there is an awful lot we need to do individually to correct what we each contribute to the current problem by our carelessness and thoughtlessness in the course of wasteful activities and misconceived pleasure. We should be sure we are practicing what we preach to others.

But the greatest expectation and most insistent demand of most of us now seem to be centered in what business can and should do—presumably at "business expense".

What we all need to keep firmly in mind is that the expense of what business does both in producing wanted goods and services—and in performing other acts to meet public demand or approval—is necessarily done on a something-for-something basis. And this needs especial emphasis now not only about pollution correction but also in such other "social responsibility" activities such as beautification, ghetto redemption, and providing persuasion, training and unearned pay to backward or reluctant workers.

It is mighty good of private companies to *want* to apply their *capabilities* to this needed work. It is also mighty fortunate for all concerned that the public wants or permits this work done by them rather than by gov-

151

ernment which would not do it as well or as economically.

But to the extent these activities *materially* lower overall productivity or otherwise raise costs *substantially,* the bill must and will be paid by consumers in prices higher than they would otherwise be—the only likely exception being where a company's competitors are somehow escaping their responsibilities in a big way.

For a long time on the way up with our level of living, we were happy to welcome the smokestacks and steam pollution which came with the payrolls, the local purchases, the tax-support of schools and other government activities—and the church and charity contributions—which we found so desirable for the community. And as another result, we and consumers elsewhere bought the output of that business at much, much less than would have been necessary if the pollution had been forbidden.

We see this history repeating itself now when Brazil says "come on down and pollute." They would like some of our jobs and present level of living down there.

We here have now obviously arrived at the point where our pollution demands—and both our technology and level of living permit—that we invest in considerable pollution correction at the expense of foregoing an equal value in goods and services.

We as consumers—and as direct and indirect taxpayers—need thus to keep before us our obligation to ourselves to demand from both business and government only what we are prepared to pay for in higher prices and higher taxes—or in fewer products and services—or in both.

One of the best among the good and bad of the freeze and Phase II is that we are each having to re-examine our previous ideas about where prices came from and what makes them attractive or intolerable.

Prices are now too high—and jobs too scarce—because too few of us have stopped to realize that we, as consumers, pay practically all the expenses of government as well as of any business that long survives.

Too many of us—in fact, the majority of the whole public—have gone on negligently or naively assuming that we had a more or less neutral "seat in the stands" at contests that *appeared* to be between employees and employers over more pay with no more production to match, and between government and those who wanted something-for-nothing from government.

The majority of us—as consumers—simply did not sense:

that these contests were over *our* money

that our letting pay be forced up—without more goods and services to match—was forcing *our* prices up.

that unwisely urging or neglectfully permitting our government to "give" to some or all of the public at so-called "government expense" was actually at *our* expense, and that this expense was going to show up not only in *some* more taxes *directly and visibly* levied *on us* but also in *a whole lot* more taxes *indirectly* levied *on us* both through the taxes first levied on business so they will have to be hidden by business in *price to us,* and through the *tax of inflation* which, as we now too well know, is the most brutal, the most deceitful and the most debilitating of all taxes—taxes which cannot be escaped by us consumers.

153

Let's each recognize our duty to ourselves, as well as to the country, to help all within our possible reach to understand the facts and become *our part* of a really meaningful corrective consumer movement.

UNEMPLOYMENT

In our present situation, unemployment is understandably much in the news and a source of real worry to us all.

What most of us need to keep clearly in mind is the hard fact that where a citizen wants to work on a something-for-*something* basis—and is not getting it—the reason is almost always that his services are just not worth what they would cost the ultimate consumer from whom the bill has to be collected in the end and who is the sole final arbiter of the worth in question.

We, who make up the public majority, need to realize what we are doing to ourselves when we force or even sanction higher pay without higher output to match. This always causes inflation, or unemployment, or both.

In this area, most of us are probably the worst fooled by minimum wage laws. They seem so fair and so innocent of any bad results of real consequence.

The first effect of such laws is to price out of the market so many present and prospective workers who are precisely those whom the laws are wrongly presumed to help—such, for instance, as the blacks, youth and other unskilled whom the rest of us, who are still employed, then have to support in idleness.

The second effect of these so-called minimum wage laws is to raise all the other rates which are above the minimum. The formerly ruling differentials between the various skills are simply reestablished from the bottom clear up to the top.

We of the majority also need to get the vivid picture of how this pricing pay out of the market forces employers to eliminate jobs through increasing investment in technology *much faster than is economic* for the public—and this on top of the public being also saddled with the support of the displaced in idleness.

In short, the public majority's employment policy—as implemented by the publics representatives and negligently accepted by the majority of us—is forcing employers to keep limiting their employment to those higher and higher up the skill and productivity scale just as fast as the services of the lower producers are progressively priced beyond what consumers will refund to the employers.

It is to your interest to tell your representatives and fellow citizens—and to write Judge Boldt, Chairman of the Pay Board—how you feel about this, whatever that may be.

PRODUCTIVITY

As long as productivity gains for the country were 2 to 3% a year—and wage increases were being forced up 3 to 4%—the difference going into inflation was more or less tolerable. But recent pay increases have been running two to four times any productivity increase, and the whole difference has had to go into higher unemployment, or higher prices, or—as we see—too much of both.

After we have hopefully arrested inflation, we will still have the job of deserving and securing the ever higher level of living that is both the desire and the wide-open opportunity of us all. This can and will come only from saving and investing more, then working harder or more intelligently as specialists producing more for each other, and being sure we eliminate all senseless waste in the process.

Contrary to what is being too fashionably taught and assumed, all real progress comes from some temporary self-denial in order to be able to *invest* toward the hoped-for later enjoyment of larger and more rewarding benefits. This is what we do when we go to school, protect our health, develop a reputable character, and save some money for the rainy day or brighter satisfactions.

Increased productivity *per man-hour* is one of our great hopes right now. As already indicated, this can come primarily from two sources: First, from increased investment in arm-lengthening ideas and equipment. Second, from making full use of skill, care and effort.

To come by the required investment, we must get to understand the private business process well enough to appreciate how we simply must see that people have a favorable economic, moral and political climate for the creation and investment of savings. To get the application of the required skill, care and effort, we must again understand private business well enough to appreciate that we are on a something-for-*something* basis and that, if *we* expect to get what *we* want, we simply have to offer in return an *equal value* judged from the *other fellow's* standpoint.

But increased productivity *per man hour* will not solve inflation and give us a higher level of living—*if* we let the drain from taking care of non-productive citizens increase faster than the output of the citizens still producing. Our level of living is determined by the output *per year* spread over each man, woman and child in our country.

It is to your interest to tell your representatives and fellow citizens—and to write Judge Boldt, Chairman of the Pay Board—how you feel about this, whatever that may be.

CONTROLS ALONE WILL NOT SAVE US

In a situation like we now have, most everybody welcomes the idea of controls in the beginning. For things have obviously gone wrong, and abuses need to be stopped. And we all certainly want to give our every cooperation and support to sound efforts at correction.

But too few of us stop to realize the degree to which we citizens are ourselves each responsible for the fix we are in, and will each have to pay our part of the cost of what we have unwisely done ourselves and have unwisely demanded or allowed that our representatives do.

It is the rare one of us who does not assume that he should rightly go free of any controls and that most all others are the ones the need to be controlled. We are going to be doubly shocked as it dawns on us not only that the controls do apply to us but also that we are not thereby making a personal "sacrifice" for the common good but are simply paying for our just share of the cost of our own past misled actions or of our expensive negligence as to what our representatives were doing.

After we get informed and sophisticated enough to make our representatives stop inflation and minimize unemployment, our getting back on the track to ever better material and non-material living will be our next quest. Success in this will depend on the degree to which we also improve our understanding and action in keeping with the hard fact that the level of *real* pay—and the level of living—can go up *only* as *both* the *output per man hour* goes up and the *total production* becomes more *per year* per man, woman and child in our country.

The most urgent need for improved understanding by the majority of us right now seems to be in the areas of unemployment, productivity and profit as well as of inflation.

Most of the emphasis in Washington and in the public media is on stopping or slowing that big part of our inflation which comes from the government having to print worthless extra money to put in the hands of consumers so they can buy at the higher prices made necessary by the arbitrary pay cost increases which are unmatched by increases in goods and services.

The other big source of inflation is continuing its full flow, and it can more than offset any downward pressure on inflation from the corrections now being sought in the unwarranted pay increases.

This other source is the government's printing of worthless extra money to pay for those goods and services which the public majority wants or permits some or all of the public to receive at so-called "government expense".

It is obvious that most citizens do not realize that what government spends has to be collected in the end from tax-paying consumers—(1) *directly* as visible taxes, or (2) *indirectly* and invisibly either in the form of taxes *supposedly* levied on business but necessarily having to be included in the prices business has to charge to consumers in order to survive, or in the form of the *tax of inflation* which as we see is the most brutal, the most deceitful and the most debilitating of all taxes.

So our public majority today too loosely assumes that the money for what government supplies is going to come from someone or somewhere else. That majority would flatly refuse to pay visibly or knowingly for lots of things the government does and for the enormous waste they see going on in the process.

Thus our government—believing it *politically* necessary to appear to be doing what the majority of its constituents demands or allows—is driven by the public's false expectations to resort to the deceitful process of collecting the cost from that same unsuspecting public through the tax of inflation hidden in consumer prices.

What we each need to do is to discuss this with all within our possible reach—and then see that we and they not only stop urging or permitting such actions by our government but also go beyond and convince our representatives that it is no longer "good politics" back home for them to engage further in these deceitful and damaging practices.

TWO WAYS TO COLLECT GARBAGE

In New York City there are two groups of workers who collect garbage—the municipal sanitation crews and the private carters who serve about 125,000 business locations.

The collection cost per ton of the City Sanitation Department is $49. The tax-paying, profit-making private carters do the job for $17.50—about 35% of the City cost.

In 1970, the taxpayers' cost of the "nonprofit" municipal service was about $180 million. This indicates that private enterprise could have saved the people of New York City about $120 million, according to the figures of The American Economic Foundation.

Private garbage collectors operate 980 trucks, about 95% of which are operable at any given time. The City operates 1,850 trucks, of which only about 65% are usually operable. In other words, private enterprise keeps about 930 of its 980 trucks rolling; the City department keeps about 1,230 of 1,850 units on the streets.

159

Another similar comparison is the lesser cost of sending packages through the private, tax-paying, profit-earning United Parcel Service when compared with the government's U.S. Post Office.

Why is it that public enterprise performs so poorly?

The American Economic Foundation answers by pointing the finger at the "nature of human nature."

Most people—managers and employees—do their best only when they have to. Private enterprise must make a profit to stay in business. It has hungry competitors. It has hard-nosed, wage-conscious labor unions, and hard-nosed, profit-conscious management. They know that success depends upon satisfying hard-nosed, price-conscious customers.

As a result, both "Labor ʹ and "Capital," hopefully, know that efficiency is the price of survival.

Public enterprise is free of these disciplines. It cannot fail because deficits are paid out of taxes. Public employees almost never lose their jobs. The customer's opinion doesn't count!

BUSINESS' SHOW-&-TELL DILEMMA

Business in our economy generally does most things well. It has to, or it doesn't survive. Think of the cars, tooth pastes, and soap chips you don't see around anymore. Their manufacturers didn't do things well.

But *all* that business does isn't necessarily done as well as it might be!

For all their successes at the market place, even prosperous businesses are falling down in communicating the role that their successes—their products, their sales, their payrolls, their profits, their participation in community concerns—actually play in the comfortable way of life we've grown to expect. In short, business is sitting back, silent, while attacks from all quarters condemn the very mechanics that contribute to our well being.

For instance, G. J. Tankersley, president of East Ohio Gas Co., said recently "Many people at all levels of government actually consider it their duty to denounce profit—an ironic situation when almost all businesses pay more dollars per share to federal, state, and local governments than to their stockholders. . . ."

Talking about the gradually shaping role of tax collector that business is reluctantly taking, he said, "New taxes on business gladden political hearts and the public. (But) this money at some future date must come from the consumer in the cost of goods and services he buys."

He continued, "The old demand to tax business, not the individual, is constantly reiterated. This has to be an insult to the thinking consumer."

Business can't seem to make clear the fact that profits create new jobs, enable business to improve the quality of its products and services, provide vital tax funds for essential community services, and make possible the upgrading of employees from minority groups, control of pollution, and strides in solving other social problems.

"When profits go down," Mr. Tankersley said, "layoff lists stretch out, there are no new jobs for young men and women, and governments face financial crisis from lost tax revenues."

The problem is in communications. Any way we can make the message more understandable?

161

DOES FOREIGN TRADE
HURT EMPLOYMENT
AND ECONOMY IN
THE UNITED STATES?

The United States has had a "balance of payments" deficit for every year but two in the last 20 years, and certain political interests are attempting to fasten the blame on multinational companies.

The term, "balance of payments deficit" simply means that we've got more money going to foreign countries for the imports we buy than we have coming into the U.S.A. for the exports we sell. Naturally, a deficit in this area can't do much for business and jobs.

But to hang the blame on private enterprise for the deficit, and make it an excuse for legislation that restricts business operations overseas (as in the Hartke-Burke Bill), just isn't considering all the facts.

A look at U.S. Companies' records since 1950 shows a **surplus** in the balance of payments **every year.** Businesses have contributed a net cumulative credit of more than $71 billion to the balance of payments in that time.

Government, on the other hand, has been in **deficit** every year since 1950, resulting in a cumulative deficit in excess of $111 billion.

What's that prove? It shows that harsh legislation against multinational companies won't reverse the outflow of U.S. dollars. The flow overseas actually is the result of government expenditures; not business activities.

To restrict businesses successes would actually hurt earnings capacities for thousands of U.S. workers as well as those abroad. Companies here would have to stop manufacturing supplies and parts for their overseas locations.

OUTPUT IS SLOWING DOWN

High productivity—or output per man hour—is the basis for a growing, healthy economy and a rising standard of living, according to Carl Madden, chief economist for the U.S. Chamber Of Commerce.

In the United States we've always been used to a high level of productivity and the resulting high standard of living. We've always managed some concern for those nations with the low productivity rate and low living standards.

In our country today the productivity of the worker is still the highest in the world *but* the annual growth rate of U.S. productivity is slowing down. The rate of growth for 1965-69 is 2.5% annually. In Japan, it's 13.4%; in Holland, 10.6%; in France, 6.9%; in Germany, 6.4%; and in Great Britain, 4.3%.

That's not good news, but it helps us to understand the reasons for many of our problems in competition with foreign manufacturers and their effects on employment and economic growth in the U.S.A.

Mr. Madden concludes, "To improve our productivity and our ability to compete internationally we need more capital investment per worker in the form of more and better machines and better education and worker skills."

To this list of needs, we'll add one more big one: EFFORT! Even the machines and education and skills will go wasted if we refuse to accept the idea that *"It does* matter whether or not we work a full day and turn out a quality job."

POLLUTION AND BABY'S BATH WATER

Evidence of U.S. industry's ever growing efforts at reducing pollution and increasing reclamation of waste are being seen more and more around us. A professor emeritus at the University Of Michigan recently pointed out that the steel industry alone remelted more than 90 million tons of scrap metal in a recent year.

The paper industry reprocessed more than 20 million tons of waste paper in the same year.

The chemical industry is constantly finding new uses for its wastes, converting them into something else useful to mankind.

And so it goes, with many industries responding to the very real needs of our society to halt abuses to our land, water, and air. There's much being done—but there's much more to be done, some of it by industry, some by municipal governments, and much by individuals. Pollution control legislation is assuming an understandably high priority in Congress, but as ESB President Edward J. Dwyer pointed out in his recent talk to the Philadelphia Rotary Club (story on Page 1), "The quickest route to depression would be to curtail the use of energy, suspend construction of new power plants, and resist technological advances—all in the name of a better environment."

He points out that we all lose when "irresponsible criticism and ill-conceived legislation impair faith in, and the operation of, our economic system . . ." and that our businesses and industry "keep our economy moving, keep opening up new areas of opportunity, keep generating the private and public funds that help care for the poor, look after the sick and the aged, and clean up our air and water."

Reasonable pollution discipline through legislation is in order for both industry and individuals, but the problems of pollution control are incredibly complex in a society grown great through technology. Misguided solutions based on political gains will be dangerous.

The problems are too complicated for simple, unduly restrictive answers. A geological science professor at the University of Wisconsin recently responded to student proclamations about the subject:

" . . . Really concerned? Want to start on the energy industries now? Take off those nylon products, sell the car, turn off the heat, avoid the bus, boycott any energy-generated products (you could start with clothes, books, paper, pens, etc.) and don't have children." He concluded, "Man, not industry, is the real enemy . . . ."

In applying practical solutions, the expression "Let's not throw out the baby with the bathwater" seems to be most appropriate.

BUSINESS PROFITS & HUMAN NEEDS

Today's NEWS tell readers of the strides our Company and the battery industry have made over the last ten years. Its report on Company President Dwyer's predictions for the next decade tell of an anticipated doubling of the battery market.

More orders from customers throughout the 1970's —providing, of course, the customers select ESB-made battery products—is a welcome prediction as we start into a new year. There are no guarantees, but the long-range outlook appears bright for manufacturers of packaged power products.

In another area of interest for the Company, its president is *on record* in support businessmen's responsibilities for responding to human needs.

What are these human needs, and where do they fit into the demands on an employer's time? Mr. Dwyer told National Association Of Manufacturers Diamond Anniversary Meeting conferees that the social ills that must have the attention of businessmen include housing, education, crime prevention, environmental improvement, and equal opportunity. And he also advised, as described in the story on this Page, that the businessman can make contributions in these areas *only* after he has made a success of his company's business. Unless his business is profitable, he won't be around to make any more than a fleeting contribution to society.

During times when the business system seems directly in the gun sights of all special interest crusades, it makes sense to recognize the obligations of business in the field of social issues and, just as important, to establish the priorities for doing something about it.

STOPPING SMOKE BY BRAINS, NOT CHAINS

If we had a dictator, says NATION'S BUSINESS Magazine, he could solve our air pollution problems overnight.

He could outlaw automobiles, industrial plants, electric power, kitchen stoves, and all the other necessities that make smoke but also make our lives so healthy and comfortable.

But, of course, the American people wouldn't stand for that. It would be pretty hard to keep some guy from starting a fire to cook some food.

So, let's weigh the steps we take toward the fine goal of clean air—and clean water, too—against their cost.

We can solve our problems better with brains than with chains.

166

THE OTHER QUARTER OF YOUR PAY

The amount of your gross pay (before taxes and other deductions) really represents only about three-fourths of your actual compensation for the work that you do.

That's so because the benefit plans that are in force for you and other ESB employees cost the Company roughly about a third again the cost of wages and salaries paid out. And that's about par for all of American industry, where employee benefits (we used to call them "fringe benefits" before they became such a substantial cost) carry a price tag that has risen rapidly in recent years to more than 30% of employee compensation.

These payments to you cover things like all insurance coverages, pensions, holidays, vacations, Social Security payments, unemployment compensation payments and many more. Chances are you already know about the extra benefits your job carries, but knowing how substantial the costs for them turn out to be might make it just a little easier to absorb all the tax and Social Security deductions that show up on the "debit side" of your pay stub.

PROTECTION AND RESTRICTION

Politicians talk about "consumer protection" in a way that reminds us of the times we have been deceived by a store or have been disappointed in a product.

But there is no automatic magic by which some sort of consumer protection agency in Washington or more laws controlling the production of products can guarantee consumers' satisfaction all of the time.

Over the years the Federal Trade Commission, the

Pure Food & Drug Administration, and many other agencies at all levels of government have had the power to deal with fraud.

Some of the new, proposed legislation is directed at strengthening the powers of these agencies; some with the complete overhaul of this nation's "market place" system.

Consumer fraud is a legitimate problem. Answers must be found to protect consumers from irresponsible "cheats." But whatever is enacted must not penalize the honest and legitimate businessman. Congress should safeguard against laws that will discourage the introduction of new products, reduce the number of choices, and increase costs as a result of limited competition.

Both the businessman and the customer have a stake in it.

NEEDS HELP—BUT IT'S NOT DEAD

Ours is a nation with a conscience.

It takes time for the message of concern to sift through the millions upon millions of written and spoken words that form our communications network, but the country's social and environmental problems. seldom are ignored, once they've been recognized. If a fault must be found in our response to areas of national concern, it would probably be in our communications *over-reaction* rather than any absence of attention.

In short, we generally do something about a wrong, once it is acknowledged. Often, however, we are susceptible to exaggerated claims on behalf of what really are reasonable and justifiable complaints.

One such example concerns pollution. We've got pollution all right and we'd better do something about it in all segments of our society—from the local government sewage and incinerator plants down through industry and power companies and on to the private "trash tossing" citizen. But we can solve the problem without an exaggeration such as *"Lake Erie is dead."* We've heard the statement and we've come to accept it as an example of the need for urgent action.

Action on Lake Erie is needed all right, but the lake isn't dead! Actually, Lake Erie is producing one half of the fish catch of all the five Great Lakes. Fifty million pounds of fish per year are being brought in from Lake Erie, and that's about the same amount produced in 1878, when catches were first recorded.

Here's another fact: Sixty-five percent of sulfur compounds and 99% of hydrocarbons entering the atmosphere each year are from natural, not man-made sources.

There are problems in our society and we've got to solve them. But let's approach them rationally, and not hysterically.

HEALTHY AMERICAN BUSINESS IS VITAL TO YOU!

Under a headline reading, "American Business Can Sell Anything Except Its Most Important Product—ITSELF," the Warner & Swasey Company in Cleveland states that "The most important thing in America today to the safety and well-being of every American is solvent, healthy American business."

The statement appeared in recent issues of news-type magazine publications. Think about the statement. Here is the reasoning:

WHEN business is sick, all America is sick—charity and education shrink, wages disappear for millions, savings evaporate, young people get no jobs, opportunities and hope disappear, neighborhoods sink into slums.

WHEN business is prosperous there are more and more jobs, charity is extended, more profits produce more taxes for more education and other good uses, opportunities increase for all the young, modern housing gets built.

THAT'S how vital healthy, prosperous business is to the well-being of all America. But you don't often hear American business men pointing out that fact.

THEY'D better.

WE'LL BET YOUR ANSWER IS WRONG!

Try this question on your family—and your neighbor, too:

"What do you estimate is the percent of profit on each dollar of sales the average manufacturer makes after taxes?"

Some economists who care about our free enterprise structure are deeply concerned at responses to this question by the average American. They are startled to find how uninformed the public is about the workers' and the companies' claims on the sales dollar.

What about you?

What do you estimate the percent of profit on each sales dollar to be? Do you figure between 25 and 30%? If you do, you're right on the button with the response given by the general public in recent surveys. The average estimate was 28%.

That "28 cents" figure is the average estimate, *but the right figure is 4 cents per dollar.* That's correct.

170

Only 4% of sales goes to the manufacturer as profit.

Profit margins today actually are close to the lowest level in a quarter of a century.

Seems really inappropriate at this time for one of the major "voices of the labor movement" to declare that the workingman is shouldering the brunt of Phase II restrictions (on wages) while business continues its "unfair profit." His statement finds warm reception from those who think that business is gobbling up 28 cents in profit on each sales dollar—but at a 4¢-rate can we be swayed by loud speeches?

We think it's not likely when employees actually get many times as much in the form of wages and salaries. (Last year at ESB, for instance, costs of employee earnings and benefits were nine times as much as profits!)

PROFITS—AND YOU

They created your job and help
assure that it won't disappear

Nowadays profits are under attack. Many people just don't seem to understand why they're essential. Of course, *we* know that if the company doesn't make a reasonable profit, our jobs may just fade away.

But it's not enough for us just to know this. We must spread the word. When someone tries to tell you that profits aren't necessary, be ready with the straight facts. It's really a simple story: Profits provide the funds to expand business, to create jobs, to keep our economy moving ahead.

Critics make much of the total volume of corporate profit. They are quick to point out that 1970's manufacturing profit was $28.6 billion. They tell the world that this is an awful lot of money, and so it is.

But they neglect to tell the whole story—that this figure represents only 4 per cent on total sales and that this profit margin was the lowest in 20 years. They neglect to tell the important fact that only out of profit can come plant expansion and new job opportunities. That only out of profit can come the funds to train the undertrained. That only out of profit can come the research, technology and hardware which will permit solutions to our environmental problems.

Today critics of the profit system are calling for control of profits. Yet, at the same time they are asking business to make great commitments to help save the cities and in other areas of social responsibility.

Unless a business is operating profitably, it cannot assure its employees of their jobs—much less take on new social responsibilities.

It's high time for all of us to become active defenders of the profit system. Our jobs are at stake!

Profit is not a *cost* to the consumer, but *benefits* the consumer through achieving prices which are less then they would be if it were not for the profit-induced incentive to compete, to invest in improvements, and to manage efficiently.

Profit does not cause inflation, but *reduces* the amount of inflation there would otherwise be.

Profit is not "stolen", but is the *earned* reward for efficiently supplying what customers want within a price at which less efficient competitors (the majority) are constantly going broke.

Profit is not the worker's enemy, but his best friend. For ⅛ of what is left after paying all *outside* expenses—the other ⅞ going to the worker—the investor supplies the arm-lengthening ideas and equipment which so largely take the work out of work, multiply the human output many times, and result in the 7/8 buying so much.

There is no job security like working for a steady earner of profit adequate not only to promote sales at the currently competitive prices required but adequate also to warrant investment in growth and improvement which will enable to producer to keep up with—or ahead of—his domestic and foreign competition.

Profit is not "huge" or "exhorbitent" or "swollen", but is surprisingly small not only compared with what others get from a business but also compared with the investors' contribution in doing typically 95% of the work for 5% of the sales dollar.

Profit does not go to just some few, but goes *directly* to about 50,000,000 investors—involving half our families—and also *indirectly* to practically every man, woman and child in the U.S.

In short, profit is the driving force toward the greatly desired growth of *jobs* in numbers, inattractiveness, in promotional opportunities, in *real* pay, and in job security. Profit is the driving force likewise toward attractive value in wanted goods and services, and is even the poor man's best friend.

May we suggest that you will be serving your own interests—plus the public's—in sharing this corrective information with your representatives and your fellow citizens.

INDUSTRY OVERPAID?
Many Americans Say YES—
But Facts Say Otherwise

How much profit do various people think the average

When various types of people were asked how much the average manufacturer makes in profits in the U.S. today, the guess ranged from 21 cents to 38 cents on each dollar. No group was even close to the facts . . . that the average profit, after taxes, is only 4 cents on each dollar. Profits are the key to the success of the American way of doing business. Profits create jobs. If there were no profits, companies could not buy additional equipment, build new plants, and develop new products.

"LOOK! THAT'S OUR MONEY THEY'RE SPENDING."

History strongly supports the thesis that public expenditures will always increase sufficiently to pre-empt every increase in public revenues. In short, government will spend all the money the taxpayers cough up—and then some. So, it's obvious that far more rigorous devices are required if the rate of expenditure growth is to be moderated. Scheduled, periodic reduction in income tax rates over the years may prove to be the only effective way to control the uptrend in government spending.

Anyone who thinks the situation isn't serious should consider this—it has been predicted that the Federal budget by fiscal 1976 would rise to between $312 billion and $325.7 billion.

Less than 60 days after Congress convened for the recent session, bills which would cost taxpayers more than $130 billion were introduced. If the costs were added to the present budget, it would mean additional spending of nearly 60 per cent.

So, taxpayers, look sharp. Yes, look into that famous edifice in Washington and see what is going on there. It is your money that is being spent so fast.

IT'S UP TO US

*We must increase productivity
to cut down inflation*

Probably the most profound problem facing our country's economy today is that of inflation. Every citizen—businessman, worker and consumer alike—has felt its direct effect through higher prices and higher taxes.

Who gains, then? Actually, not the businessman, whose pricing policies are governed by competition while being faced with increasing costs; nor the wage earner, who soon finds that his newly enlarged pay check is shrinking from increased prices and taxes. Governmental units, too, whether local, state or federal, find themselves in financial crises due to increased operating expenses and finance costs.

The answer, then, is that none of these groups gains as a whole over the long run. Such gains as are made must be considered temporary, since the next round of increases in costs, prices and taxes wipes them out. This is true for all who operate within the American enconomy. The only possible winners are from without—foreign competitors who have the advantage of lower labor costs—and they have already established substantial footholds . . .

Since inflation affects all segments of our economy, it is to the benefit of all to bring it under control. Actually, both management and labor have a stake in pursuing policies that will help moderate the problem. The alternative for not doing so is continuing inflation, deterioration of U.S. industry's ability to compete with imports and resultant unemployment.

By far the best solution is increased productivity, which by definition means the reduction of labor costs per unit of production.

For management this means setting production schedules so maximum efficiency can be attained, reducing overtime requirements to absolute necessities and providing the best tools and facilities possible.

For labor it means doing a fair day's work, being on the job every day, and reducing scrap and the need for repair work.

OUR REPUTATION

*Pride in the company helps
future growth and progress*

Have you ever thought of the importance of our company's reputation? Or what it is that builds that reputation?

It has been said that a company's reputation is its most precious asset—and rightly so, for it is built by the people who work for the company. If a company's reputation is good, it instills confidence . . . the company grows . . . it provides more security . . . more opportunity for the people within the company.

We are fortunate because those who have been here before have set high standards of quality, service and value. They built the reputation which serves as a foundation for us.

We now have the opportunity to use this reputation as a base for greater growth. Upon this base we can expand our distribution and increase our business. The result: more opportunity and security for each of us.

But to achieve this opportunity, this security, we must always keep in mind that our reputation must be maintained and must be improved upon. If it is not, the foundation will crumble and with it will go the benefits.

What is it that has built the reputation which we must work to maintain?

It has been a company desire, in fact a company dedication, to provide our customers with the best possible service at the lowest possible rates.

How can each of us, individually, contribute to the continued growth of our reputation?

It means paying attention to the means by which we go about our jobs as well as the ends which we hope to attain. It includes such things as making suggestions . . . finding new ways to do the job better . . . increasing efficiency . . . eliminating waste . . . becoming a salesman for company service, policies and principles.

As we do all these things, we shall enjoy our work more. We shall build a greater pride in our company and its reputation. And we shall instill this same enthusiasm and pride in others who join our organization as we progress and grow in the future.

Don't Let
Recreation

MAKE YOU A WRECK!

Protect yourself. Safety is a year round vigil. Remember you are safer on the job than away from it.

Traveling by car. The first rule is to make sure the car is in perfect shape—tires, batteries, windshield wipers, mirrors, lights, radio for weather warnings.

Check your insurance and auto club protection, particularly if you are planning to leave the country. Things to keep in the car: first aid kit, flashlight and flares, fire extinguisher, sunglasses. If you are taking the kids, make up a list of few simple rules to be obeyed when the car is in motion, such as (1) Fasten seat belts. (2) Do not load up back deck with stuff which may obstruct driver's view or slide off on passengers. (3) No shouting or singing without driver's permission.

Comfort and peace of mind. If you must have glasses to drive or read, do you have a spare pair or a prescription? Travel light and avoid risk of loss. If you are taking medication be sure you have enough and also copies of the prescriptions. Be sure to keep a list of the numbers in case of loss just as you do for your travelers checks. Split the responsibility for carrying valuables and also give each traveler some cash and change in case of separation or accident, or as a time saver so that errands can be accomplished efficiently. Relax—have fun!

"FAT CATS" ARE WHO—
AND HOW MANY?

As you see in the press and on TV, claims are being made by some top union officials that Phase II has been designed to benefit only a *few* "fat cats" who profit from business.

The facts are that—at this writing—the unio uncials have won all the battles but the retroactivity one, and have even won that one partially.

But let's look at the "fat cats" in question. Who are they, and how many are there?

The answer is that a good 50 million citizens are *direct* owners of private business. This represents half our families, including probably half of the 80 million employees and their families.

The answer is also that, in addition, there are further millions of *indirect* investors with savings at risk in business obligations whose yield, worth and safety depend on the ability of business to offer attractive values while keeping competitive and solvent. These obligations represent pension funds, insurance policies and annuities, savings bank accounts and open bank deposits, and the holders obviously include *all* the work force as well as practically every other man, woman and child in our country.

A privately owned business is a sort of clearinghouse where people voluntarily come together—as specialists—*to do things for each other*. Investors, customers, employees, suppliers and neighbors associate to make contributions and claim rewards equal in value to their contributions. They so associate because they can thus *do more* for each other as a result of the way the contributions of owners and managers—in ideas, designs, materials, facilities, coordination, subdivision of operations, opportunity for specialization, and risk-taking ability and willingness—so "lengthen the arms" of the individual contributor that his output is many times what it would be if he were working independently with the aid of only the ideas, materials, tools, facilities, skills and other resources he could personally bring to the work.

Incidentally, after all the other expenses have been paid, what is left for the employees and owners to divide between themselves is typically divided ⅞ to the employees and only ⅛ to the owners. For this ⅛ the investor has taken most of the work out of work, has created fairly steady jobs and good consumer values, and has done 95% of the work for 5% of the sales dollar—with about half this 5% having to go back into the business to make up for inadequate depreciation allowance and to improve competitiveness and thus serve consumers while saving jobs.

Let's appreciate the degree to which *all* of us are "fat cats".

LEAPFROGGING FOR YOU?

One of the toughest assignments we the public have imposed on the Pay Board is to try to eliminate the "leapfrogging" enemy to our being able to hold inflation to 3% by holding pay rises to 5.5% and price rises to 2.5%.

This leapfrogging source of senselessly higher prices and lower employment is not an invention. It is rather a Rube Goldberg type of assembly—or a Topsy-like growth—of ratcheting, pattern-setting, hope-building and hope-dashing regamorale. Most of us are naive indeed for not having long since recognized what needless

180

damage was thereby being done to us as workers, consumers and savers.

What has been going on—and what has helped greatly to bring on our present pay and price inflation crisis —is substantially this:

One union official imposes on a pattern-setting employer a highly inflationary and job-killing settlement which goes way ahead of even the already so distorted pay scale. He does so on usually four excuses: (1) That he did not get what was equitable or even what was promised the last time, and is entitled to an adjustment now to correct this, (2) that he has fallen further behind the contract parade since his last settlement two or three years ago despite the contracted quarterly cost-of-living raises and yearly "improvement factor" raises, and he needs a second added adjustment to make up for the inadequacies and also for what his competing fellow union officials have gotten meanwhile, (3) that the country is faced with a more sharply rising cost-of-living rate over the period of the new contract, and he must have a third added adjustment to provide against this in advance to match what his fellow union officials will be getting over that period, and (4) that he must have a fourth substantial ingredient added with which to adjust the inevitable "inequities"

A week or a month later, the next union official imposes on a pattern setter in another industry a still more preposterous inflating settlement first, because it has become the pleasant requirement of status, in this competitive political game, that each new contract must "get more" than the last settlement made by a fellow official, and second because he usually finds it actually very necessary politically with his members to take back what looks like an answer to past cost of living increases and to providing for future cost-of-living increases the members do not realize they are bringing on themselves as well as creating for others.

The next official acts the same way—and the next—and so on until the vast difference thus generated between pay rises and any productivity rises are showing up in the misunderstood cost-of-living rises from this source along with the rises from the government supplying the public with goods and services the public will not knowingly pay for.

What the public majority needs to do is to insist on its representatives in unions, government and business slowing down and evening up this process to the point where the traditional market relationships between various skills are restored and where general pay increases (including any so-called "cost-of-living" adjustment) do not total more than the productivity increases.

PROFIT DESPERATELY
NEEDS YOUR HELP

There can no longer be any doubt that the new inflation of the late 60's, the freeze, and Phase II to date have all worked against profit being substantial enough either to reward present investments equitably or to create the ability and willingness to save and invest the further funds so needed now for the accomplishment of more attractive consumer values for the benefit of the whole public.

We simply have to face the fact that politicians in unions and in government find profit a very popular whipping boy. Profit has been going down for the past five years while inflationary pay went up spectacularly. Now *pay* can go on further up artificially by 5.5% a year, plus all sorts of adjustments for "catch-ups," "inequities" and other *politically* good reasons for exception. But *profit* is to get no 5.5 artificially raised ceiling and no "catch-ups," and even earned profit is to be held within the recently depressed rate.

The resulting damage to the public interest comes about simply because the public majority has let it become "good politics" for the majority's representatives in unions and in government to act that way. Phase II, *in concept,* is just as good as permitted by what was "good politics" at the moment and, *in administration,* it is going to prove just as good or bad as what is "good politics" with the majority will make it. And if it does not prove *pretty* good, the successor Phase III is going to be a whole lot rougher on citizens not only as investors but also as earners, consumers, home owners, and hopeful seekers after the better life generally.

If the politicans are reasonably correct about what the public wants or will permit—and they usually are—then it is pretty obvious that the public majority has not recently been—and is not now—equipped with the proper economic knowledge, moral fortification, and political sophistication to enable it to make decisions and take actions which really serve its own interests.

We owners of business securities and other private property are especially obligated—in our very selfish interest as well as patriotically in our country's interest—to master the full range of the facts as to the good which investment and profit do for all, and then to help all within our possible reach to be similarly grounded beyond any chance of being fooled by satans quoting perverted scripture for their purposes.

One thing you can do, with enormous multiplier effect, is to persuade every bank, retailer, and telephone, electric and gas utility within the span of your influence to *do his part,* by including corrective envelope stuffer of 3 to 4 hundred words:

1. With every weekly pay check,
2. With every monthly statement, and
3. With every quarterly dividend.

The intentional and unintentional enemies of business are playing for keeps with a public majority that does not understand the good which business does and how it does it. We had better hurry to help change that—or those little pieces of paper we have in our safety boxes will be valueless, and our own and our fellow citizens' other private property will also go down the drain.

PULLING TOGETHER

*Workers and businessmen have
no grounds for class warfare*

Workers and businessmen are *not* foes!

The kind of reasoning that suggested they *are* foes hasn't been practiced for several generations. Though they sometimes disagree on certain points, the fact is that both workers and businessmen are partners in production. They have to be for their mutual benefit.

But surprisingly, as new tax provisions were being considered in the Senate, some of organized labor's spokesmen assaulted provisions that would help to modernize U.S. plants. Opposition to an investment tax credit for industry (designed to stimulate business) almost took the form of by-gone class warfare.

People who are the workers of the nation today are better off than ever before in our country's history. Wages and salaries today take 90.2% of all the money that industry has left after purchase of materials and the cost of overhead. The other 9.8% goes into profits, dividends to stockholders, and payment for new equipment to keep jobs going.

There just are no grounds for class warfare, and it's plain to see that the men and women employed by industry today have as much at stake as the businessmen who manage the companies. All are dependent upon their companies' successes.

Incentives to encourage new factories and new equipment boost prospects for jobs and job security.

If business goes down the drain, jobs will go along with it.

Encouragement to strengthen business is the realistic position for those who depend upon its success!

WHO PAYS THE BILL—YOU?
Do you deserve to?

As you must have seen in the press and on TV, the Pay Board had to surrender to superior union authority. The public members of the Board figured the resulting added employment cost at 16.8%, or more than triple the 5.5% ceiling established for post-freeze raises.

The industry members took the position that over 4% of this added cost of the agreement was to make the welfare fund solvent and related to costs and benefits which occurred prior to the freeze, and thus would not only have been allowable any time but also would not "flow through" now with any additional pattern—setting or precedent-setting influence.

Nevertheless, the coal companies are reported to figure that their previous over-all costs will be thus increased by 8.5%, and that they need their prices raised that much—which again, is more than triple the 2.5% price ceiling sought.

We have no information other than what we get from

the public media. But it seems perfectly obvious that this surrender by the Board Majority—including all the members from industry—was in sober recognition of a stark reality.

That reality is that the public has allowed union forces to accumulate such economic and political power —not just over coal company managements but obviously over government and the public itself—that the government agency simply had to do as it did, or there would be no coal mined in the forseeable future.

The existing coal strike could go on indefinitely with no real economic pressure on the miners because of the aid they would get—as we have seen them and others get—from the public through the U.S. and other governments, from their own and other union strike funds, and from their savings and available credit.

With the coal piles already approaching the vanishing point, a continuance of the strike would simply cut in half our electricity, gas, trains, heat, etc., for an intolerable time to come.

This 16.8% pay cost increase—since we can expect little or probably no more coal mined than before— must all or practically all go immediately or soon into consumer prices of coal and of the goods and services supplied with the aid of coal along the way. There is just no chance of productivity or profit being able to absorb any appreciable part of this increased cost.

We the public—as earners, consumers, savers and voters—are in this fix because we have let ourselves be misled into neglecting to do ourselves—and neglecting to see that our representatives do—what should be done about harmful union monopoly which is not regulated by government, as telephone and electric monopolies are but, instead, it itself actually regulating government. We are—and will be—each paying a high price for that neglect.

THIS SHOWDOWN IS WITH *YOU*—
As Worker, Consumer, Saver

A pay rise of 26 percent in 17 months has just been imposed on helpless West Coast shippers and, through them, on our whole public.

The East Coast shippers have just had imposed on them a settlement even more highly inflationary and debilitating.

The press widely reports that West Coast workers have been ordered to "Stand by to march out as a solid
55   wha ytou can do about 7678
body with East Coast if the Pay Board cuts our negotiated settlement by as much as one cent."

A shutdown of every port in the land would further damage our already deeply distressed foreign trade and would thereby further reduce employment and further raise the cost of living. And this is only in addition to the inflation and unemployment the settlement would otherwise cause.

If a foreign super-power blockaded our ports, we would recognize we were at war and we would fight.

If our ports should now be blockaded by a domestic super-power in the form of an overpaid and featherbedding union, we likewise should recognize we are at war and should fight to protect ourselves as workers, consumers and savers.

Next week the Pay Board faces the decision to reduce these two settlements or to let them ride through and do their damage. The Board is a public agency and knows what it decides must have majority public understanding, approval and support—or the decision will be upset.

This threatened shutdown is a showdown—a showdown not with the employers or the Pay Board or the

government, but with you. Tell your representatives—and wire the Pay Board—that you demand
these two settlements be appropriately cut in your own
and the common interest.

TOPICAL INDEX

189

190

191